BORN ᵀᴼ BE WILD

HUNDREDS OF FREE NATURE
ACTIVITIES FOR FAMILIES

HATTIE GARLICK

PHOTOGRAPHS BY NANCY HONEY

giving
nature
a home

rspb

B L O O M S B U R Y
LONDON · OXFORD · NEW YORK · NEW DELHI · SYDNEY

giving nature a home

The RSPB is the UK's largest nature conservation charity, inspiring everyone to give nature a home so that birds and wildlife can thrive again.

By buying this book you are helping to fund the RSPB's conservation work.

If you would like to know more about the RSPB, visit their website at www.rspb.org.uk, write to the RSPB, The Lodge, Sandy, Bedfordshire, SG19 2DL or call 01767 680551.

Bloomsbury Publishing Plc

50 Bedford Square
London
WC1B 3DP
UK

1385 Broadway
New York
NY 10018
USA

www.bloomsbury.com

BLOOMSBURY and the Diana logo are trademarks of Bloomsbury Publishing Plc

First published 2016

British Library Cataloguing-in-Publication Data
A catalogue record for this book is available from the British Library.

Library of Congress Cataloguing-in-Publication data has been applied for.

ISBN: PB: 978-1-4729-1533-7
ePub: 978-1-4729-1534-4

2 4 6 8 10 9 7 5 3

Design by Gridlock Design
Illustrations by Dave Saunders
Printed and bound in China by C&C Offset Printing Co.,Ltd

MIX
Paper from
responsible sources
FSC® C008047

CONTENTS

ABOUT US

We are Hattie, Tom, Johnny and Frida. Hattie is a journalist, Tom a carpenter. Johnny splits his time between deep-sea diving and firefighting, while Frida's studies are currently concentrated on learning to walk.

In our outdoor adventures we are joined by a gangly gang that includes, amongst others Max, an aspiring spaceman, Barney, who hates peas, Ella, whose favourite colour is purple, Dylan, who is a superhero, Morenike, who wants to be a vet, Jasmine, who loves her Nintendo DS, and Remi, who sews her own clothes.

We live an (overly) busy life in an (overly) crowded, scruffy terrace in a big city. We like living this way. But we also love escaping every now and again, making a bit of space within it, and finding the weeds growing between paving slabs or the creatures living beside railway tracks.

All the activities in this book have been tested by us – mostly in areas where you are more likely to tread on discarded takeaway boxes than wild flowers. We hope you enjoy them as much as we have done.

INTRODUCTION

Want to save cash, your children's imaginations and possibly even the planet? This is the handbook you need.

All right, I know that sounds a little ambitious, but stick with me. This book is written by a parent. Not the pristine, perfect kind, either. Far from it. One who is neither an Earth Mama making her own yoghurt from a yurt nor a countess with a country pile in the Cotswolds. One who has real kids – the kind who throw tantrums and worship at the altar of the Sky box. One whose views are punctuated by high-rise buildings, not rolling hills. One who takes shortcuts and makes mistakes (a lot). One who curses creatively under her breath (occasionally).

So relax. This book will not judge you for letting Netflix babysit for the fourth afternoon in a row. It will not expect you to trek miles into pristine forest or conjure up complex yet cute craft projects. It won't expect your family life to resemble a *Hello* magazine shoot, parents to be domestic gods and goddesses, or children to be cherubs.

This book is your friend. It sets out – clearly – the magical materials nature lays on, for free, each season for families to let their legs and imaginations run wild with. From summer feathers to autumn berries, it matches this treasure with a few ordinary household items that make it easy to explore, mess around with and learn about them, and then... let the wild adventuring begin.

This book thinks the ideas kids come up with are generally more imaginative and ingenious than those that adults prescribe for them – so it's a parent's job to provide the tools and spark the imagination, then either join in the jollity or sit back and relax, ideally with a magazine and some form of beverage.

Because this book cares about you, it also provides hundreds of fun activities and simple instructions, for those times when your creativity needs a bit of a kickstart. Activities for mini Matisses, activities for small scientists. Adventures that take ten minutes, and ones that absorb whole afternoons. Projects that require only an urban balcony and ones to do in your nearest bit of real wilderness; experiments that can be made simple or complex according to age and attention span.

But remember: this book is not telling you what to do. It would not dare. These activities are jumping off points. Pursue them to the letter if you like. Or follow your kids in whatever wild and wonderful twists and turns they take.

The promise? It's easy on your wallet, easy on the planet and, most importantly, easy to have fun, together, as a whole family. Because, as Thoreau said, 'All good things are wild and free'. Or, as those other great philosophers, Steppenwolf, titled their magnum opus, 'Born to be wiiiiiiiiiiild'.

TEN TIPS FOR TURFING YOUR KIDS OUT OF THE HOUSE (HAPPILY)

1   **Take sustenance** Getting caught in a wood or park (or anywhere, really, beyond a ten-step radius of your kitchen) without an emergency packet of raisins, breadsticks, sarnies or the occasional Kit-Kat is a grievous error. Sugar is the devil, sure, but sometimes it's better the devil you know will keep your kid walking all the way back to the car, than the devil you know will emerge from within him when tired tantrums hit. Same goes for drinks. If you're leaving the house for more than an hour, a thermos in winter and a water bottle in summer are essentials.

2   **Stay warm and dry** Nothing screams 'ill prepared' louder (or just screams louder in general) than children whose parents have forgotten to dress them for the weather. If you aren't windproof and waterproof in winter, or shaded and cool in summer, your fun will be fleeting. So wear wellies, warm socks and hats, layers and waterproofs in the cold months. In the warm months equip yourself with sun hats, jelly shoes and loose cotton clothes. Oh, and remember to all wear long sleeves and trousers if you're doing battle with nettles or brambles. Ditto suncream in sunny weather.

3   **Beware of competing toys and technology** Nature's appeal is powerful but subtle. You can't really ask it to compete with an iPad or plastic toys. It's not a fair fight. So leave all that stuff behind when you venture out. Otherwise you risk being mesmerised by nature while your child is hypnotised by YouTube. Books, though, are always a good idea. Pack one to read aloud to small children under the trees, or for older children to open themselves in a rare oasis of calm. If it's one about nature, so much the better.

4   **Be flexible** You may have fixed ideas about an educational exploration of the anatomy of a dandelion. But if the child with you wants to pound it into a pulp with a potato masher instead, before smearing it across a piece of coloured paper, you must abandon your plan *immediately* unless you want to drive yourself completely and irreparably insane.

BORN TO BE WILD

5 **Three's a crowd** But in the best possible way. The more kids you herd up for each outdoor adventure, the merrier and longer their fun will be (and the less chivvying will be required).

6 **Never underestimate kids** It can be scary watching the centre of your world disappear, wobblingly, into the highest branches of a tree, or wielding a big stick in his small hand. Sensible precautions must always be taken. But remember: your children are more capable and creative than most people give them credit for (they have your genes, after all).

7 **But don't be too ambitious** It's an equally big mistake to ask too much of your family. Young children have short legs and, sometimes, short attention spans, so a bit of planning is required. Ask a four-year-old to walk miles along a dull path before the fun even begins and you will have only yourself to blame when the meltdown ensues.

8 **Forget 'perfect'** We're not aiming for 'polished' or 'perfect' here. Whether it's a raft built from sticks, a den or a quill pen, the finished project is, really, beside the point. Without wanting to sound too much like a hippy, it's about the journey, man.

9 **Collect** Everything in life can be improved simply by incorporating a treasure hunt into it. Every time you leave the house you are on a mission to uncover the most beautiful, most bizarre, shiniest or brightest natural object. When you've found it, pocket it, and add it to a dedicated display when you get home (a window ledge, shelf or fireplace swept of the usual household detritus will do nicely). Remember to collect responsibly. Have a look at our Ten Commandments on page 12.

10 **Have fun, together** One of the greatest thing about nature – one of the things that sets it apart from almost all other activities, toys, TV shows and theme parks – is that it doesn't come with an 'age-appropriate' sticker slapped on it. It's for everyone. Muck in together, marvel at its delightful or disgusting features with one another, and make the most of the magic that happens in each other's company.

THE TOOLKIT

Some people would have you believe you need specialist, cumbersome, fiddly or expensive kit to explore or make things in nature: compasses, head torches, easels and posh paints. That's fine if you are Bear Grylls or even Martha Stewart. Otherwise, can I point you in the direction of your kitchen cupboard?

Every single activity in this book can be carried out if you have the ordinary household items listed on the opposite page. Collect everything for your toolkit and find a place it can live in your house. All the items in your toolkit are things you're likely to have already, stuffed in the back of a cupboard or under the sink. Lots are bits of 'rubbish' you can recycle. Everything else can be picked up for the princely sum of a quid from your local pound store.

So here's what you do:
1   Flick to the relevant season – autumn, for example – and turn to the natural material you all want to explore, such as acorns. At the beginning of each of those sections, you'll find a short selection of the objects you'll need for those activities.
2   Spend 30 seconds collecting the objects you need from your complete toolkit and chuck them into a bag.
3   Leave the house.
4   Find your acorns (or whatever).
5   Open your bag, grab your toolkit and poke, pound, stick, paint and mash the acorns as your imaginations dictates, or use the activities in the acorns (or any) section to inspire you all.

With the toolkit at their disposal, your rabble can either collaborate on a master plan or split off individually, using different parts of it to do and make different things, at their own level. The beauty of it is this: on any given day, in any given pair of hands, one set of tools and natural materials can result in a million different projects.

Some will come from the book, some from the children's brains; some will be easy, others elaborate; some chaotic, some controlled; some fastidious, some filthy. As well as activities using items from your toolkit, you'll also find a few yoga-inspired activities scattered through the book, for when your bodies or minds need a gentle stretch.

The complete toolkit

Scissors

Coloured paper

Coloured pens and crayons (non-toxic)

Paints (non-toxic)

Brushes

Sellotape

Double-sided sticky tape

String

Blu-tack

Needle and thread

Pencil

Tissue paper

PVA glue

Food dyes

Foil takeaway containers (just rinse and store
a couple after you've eaten)

Magnifying glass

Rubber band

Empty jam jars with lids (one or two will do to
start with)

Trowel

Old sheet / scraps of white material

Paper plate

Plastic cup

Large plastic bag

Old plastic bottle

Marker pen

Skewer

Birdseed

Tray or bin liner

Measuring tape

Old cardboard scraps (bits of boxes will do)

Drinking straw

Torch

Plain paper

Card

Salt

Knife

Plastic straws

Watch / stopwatch

Towels

Candles

Ribbons

Yoghurt pots

Bucket and spade

This is all you will *need*, but that's not to say you shouldn't accessorise your own toolkit if the mood takes you. If, like a member of our family who will remain nameless, someone wants to wear a head torch and a wetsuit and carry a compass every time you leave the house, who are you to judge them?

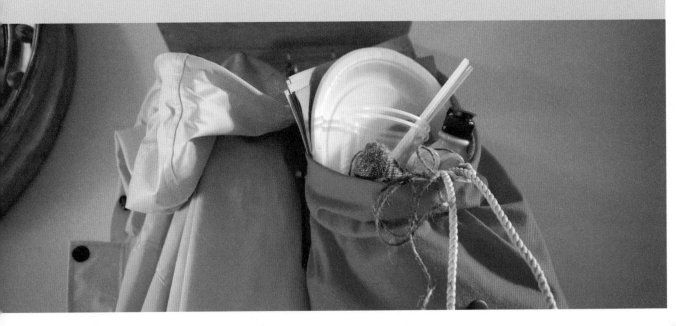

THE BENEFITS (THE GOOD, THE BAD AND THE UGLY)

We all know – in a vague, instinctive kind of way – that nature is 'A Good Thing', right? Even if, like so often in my family, life has a habit of getting in the way and, suddenly, weeks have passed without us noticing it much.

Cast your mind back to the times when you've been happiest; when the whirling noise, speed and distractions of life have stilled for a moment and – as in the calm at the centre of a storm – you've been, well, exactly that. You've just *been you*, without any disturbance or stress. You weren't – probably – checking Facebook while simultaneously sending a text message, listening to a tune and watching TV. You were – probably – outside.

For me, that's a good enough reason to try and spend as much time as possible outside as a family. Under an open sky, even in our scruffy local park, we are kinder to each other. We give each other more breathing space, in the figurative as well as the literal sense. We bicker less, laugh more. We stand taller, breathe deeper, move faster. We are all more focused, too. It's as if our attention spans stretch out across the wider horizons.

If, however, you need more than that to propel you to the front door, there's a persuasive and growing body of research into nature's benefits, particularly on kids. So here comes the science bit.

THE GOOD

- Eighty per cent of the UK's happiest people say they have a strong connection with nature, compared to under 40 per cent of the happiest.

- A survey by Play England busted the myth that modern children prefer to play indoors with technology. When asked about their favourite places to play, 88 per cent of children in the survey said they preferred a beach or river, and 79 per cent said the park. Ball games, bike riding and tree climbing were also far more popular than playing computer games.

- When Kings College London conducted a review of the relevant research, it concluded that children who learn in natural environments 'perform better in reading, mathematics, science and social studies'.

- Research into teenagers' free time, conducted for Natural England in 2006, has suggested that time spent in nature can result in better self-image, self-confidence, social skills and ability to deal with uncertainty'.

- Several studies suggest that contact with nature can lessen aggressive behaviour.

- Even the smallest contact with nature has an effect: a ten-year study in a hospital in Pennsylvania found that patients whose windows looked out onto trees required fewer painkillers, had slightly fewer complications and left hospital earlier than those with views of a brick wall.

THE BAD

- Two out of three UK parents believe their kids have less freedom to roam than free-range chickens do.

- The average American child spends as few as 30 minutes a day in unstructured outdoor play, and more than seven hours a day in front of a screen.

- Only 10 per cent of children in the UK regularly played in natural places in 2009, compared to 40 per cent in the 1970s.

- In 2014, a survey of over 2,000 schoolchildren across the UK found that 35 per cent had never been to the countryside.

- According to a 2008 National Trust survey: a third of British children could not identify a magpie; half could not tell the difference between a bee and a wasp; but 90 per cent could recognise a Dalek.

THE UGLY

- In the UK, three in ten children aged between the ages of two and 15 are now either overweight or obese, while in the US obesity rates among six to 11 year olds have more than doubled in the last two decades.

- The number of children in the US being diagnosed with a mental disorder has been rising for over a decade. Up to 20 per cent of US children now suffer from a mental disorder.

- In the UK, the use of medication to treat Attention Deficit Hyperactivity Disorder rose by more than 50 per cent between 2007 and 2012, when 657,000 prescriptions were issued in a single year.

- Statistics indicate that one in ten children and young people in the UK have a mental health illness. Four per cent of those suffer from an emotional disorder like anxiety or depression.

THE TEN COMMANDMENTS

(or: some general guidelines for nurturing nature instead of knocking it about)

Respect all wildlife However small the creature, the aim is to never scare, squash, stomp or swat it. Outside, you'll sometimes find yourself a guest in a creature's home so keep your eyes open for your hosts, act nice and use your manners.

Respect private property Whether it's a field or a front garden, if it belongs to someone else, leave it be. Imagine how you'd feel if someone wandered into your tenderly tidied home and started hacking out sections of your curtains and pulling the stuffing out of the sofa. Then imagine how livid your mother-in-law would be. That's roughly how cross farmers and home owners will be if you mess with the outdoor spaces they love.

Respect public spaces, too These, obviously, you can use, but remember that others will want to enjoy them after you, so be thoughtful about both what you remove and what you leave behind. You might see a beautiful natural collage, redolent with symbolism of the changing seasons. They might see a huge, muddy mess in the middle of their picnic spot.

Read and respect signs Personally, I'd gleefully fling every 'no ball games' notice in the land onto a bonfire. But most signs are there for a reason. Follow the rules and no one will interrupt your fun.

Be considerate of other users That couple attempting to have a romantic picnic near you in the park might not find the mood improved by the screeched sound effects of your mud fight. Or the splattering. Be kind and keep it down – or better still, find a new spot.

Leave things as you found them It's generally best to 'leave no trace' or make sure, before you go home, that the spot you've found looks the same as it did when you arrived. That's not always *completely* possible (if you've borrowed some fallen leaves, for example) but it's worth aspiring to it.

Take your rubbish home with you Take everything else, too: picnic remnants, tools and the art itself unless it's made from 100 per cent natural materials and can be returned to its natural setting.

Keep animals under control I could include wilder members of the family here, but really I was thinking of dogs.

Flower power Turning into a wildman (or woman) on these adventures is to be encouraged, but flower picking in the wild countryside is not, so try and picture yourself as the foraging rather than the pillaging kind of pioneer. Collecting fallen flowers, leaves, bits of twigs and broken-off bark is fine. Robbing a whole wood of bluebells isn't. And don't dig up any plants, not even to replant at home. It could be illegal.

Think: something lives here Even the scrubbiest blade of grass between two paving slabs might be called home by an animal. It's good to remember that when you're out collecting leaves, flowers, bark – anything really. The natural world belongs to you, so you should fight against anything that stands in the way of you exercising your right to use it. Before you chain yourself to the nearest tree trunk, however, remember that you share that ownership with billions of other creatures, too. So tread thoughtfully.

SPRING

'Spring is sprung. The grass is risin'. So where are all the bleedin' birds then, darlin'?'

Thankfully, there are still wonderful places in the world, lots of them, where spring literally springs into being. Where one day – after a long winter of fossilised browns and greys underfoot and frosty exhalations of breath from the lips – new life suddenly motors up, multicoloured, through the soil or stumbles into the fields on shaky legs. The people who live in these beautiful places (perhaps you) don't go hunting for signs of spring. Spring smacks them in the face every time they open the door.

If that is you, then congratulations. Sling this book and your toolkit into your rucksack, stick your feet in your boots and don't come back till the seasons change. Off you go now.

For our family, though, in a small house on the edge of the world's fifteenth largest city, it's different.

Because spring is sprung with slightly less fanfare in urban areas, its welcoming parade – all bells and whistles, glitz and glamour in the countryside – is smeared by fumes and knocked about by the traffic on its journey down the motorway towards us. By the time it limps down our road it's less pizazz, more, well… pffffft …like a slowly deflating party-balloon.

In fact, in neighbourhoods like ours, spring doesn't so much 'spring' as 'struggle up' instead, taking the form of dandelions in the cracks between paving stones or patches of nettles fringing tarmacked playgrounds. It all feels rather like the famous old quote above, borrowed and recast in a suitably urban mock cockney.

Our place isn't unusual. If you took our planet and span it back in time, Superman-style, by a hundred years and looked at the same number of people at random, you'd find only 13 of them living somewhere urban. Whirl on a bit and stop again, in 1990. Now around forty of our hundred would live somewhere urban. On again, to 2010, and suddenly urban populations are more than half of your hundred. Spin forwards into the future and it's believed that, by 2050, an astonishing nearly seven out of ten people will be city slickers.

Feeling dizzy? I am. Any wonder, then, that our connection to nature has become a little enfeebled over the last century, our collective reaction to it a bit, well… 'Meh'?

Because if we can't see nature, if we don't grow up immersed in its sights, songs and smells, why should we care about it? And what does the future hold for the birds, the bees, the grass and the trees if we don't?

That question, and a vague but unshakeable sense that something was missing, were what prompted us to begin loading up the buggy and go Hunting For Spring.

Hooray! Except... we weren't *really* sure what a Spring Hunt looked like, what kit you needed for such an expedition, which direction to set off in or even whether we would recognise spring when we found it...

So we started by holding family contests: who could count the most daisies growing in the graffiti-heavy shadows near the tow-bridge? What shapes could be spotted in the clouds when you lay on your back at the top of the slide in the local playground? We began, too, to talk to people who are doing crazy, cool or clever things that involved families and nature.

And from there, well... some ideas were sprung.

FACT BOX

- According to the United Nations, over a billion children now live in urban areas, and the numbers are rising.
- A generation ago, almost half of British children regularly played in wild places. Now, it's less than one in ten.
- In the US, only 26 per cent of mothers say their children play out of doors every day, though 71 per cent of them remember doing so themselves.
- According to a 2008 study by Play England, 50 per cent of British kids have been warned against climbing trees, while 20 per cent have been banned from playing conkers.
- A survey of 700 children found half of them unable to identify a daddy long-legs spider, an oak tree, a Blue Tit or a bluebell.

- Research by the RSPB found that 75 per cent of people who feel connected to nature have done something to improve their environmental impact in the last year, compared to significantly fewer of those who have not.
- According to research at Cornell University in 2006, the most direct route to us caring about the environment as adults is for us to take part in wild nature activities before we are 11.
- Or, as Sir David Attenborough, says: 'Nobody is going protect the natural world unless they understand it.'

GRASS

Grasslands cover somewhere between 20 and 40 per cent of the planet's land mass.

There are an estimated 11,000 species of grass worldwide, ranging from the short, militaristically mown blades of lawn grass (the natural habitat of retired sergeant majors), to waist-high reeds (the natural habitat of warblers) and world record-breaking 50m [164ft] tall bamboo (the fantasy habitat of pandas).

You're unlikely to come across pandas, but given the abundance of grass it should be easy enough for anyone anywhere to access a scrappy bit of green. *Should* be, but isn't. Not always.

Hunting out inspiration for getting outdoors, we visit a nursery school located on the second-largest housing estate in Europe. Situated in a grey, down-at-heel complex off a major road, it looks more like a crumbling office block than a place where magical things are happening for children. But that is exactly what it is.

Inside, we peer through smudged glass into a classroom where money and resources are clearly in limited supply. Many of the kids at Eastwood Day Nursery in south London live high up in the sky, in cramped, concrete tower blocks without access to any safe places to play, let alone a garden. But if cash does not abound here, passion and expertise do. At least twice a week, in all seasons and all weathers, the school bundles up these children in wellies and waterproofs and takes their classes outdoors.

The door opens and Samantha Olive leads out four small, excited figures. She bustles them into their outdoor clothes, wipes a snotty, scabbed nose and leads them down the main road to the luxurious landscaped grounds of Roehampton University – a ten-minute walk and yet a world away.

One boy examines some bugs. Another prods the grass with a stick. 'Forest School leaders will have a plan but they allow children to learn through their own interests and to lead the activities themselves' explains Samantha. 'That's a huge part of why Forest School develops their confidence and skills in such a huge way.' The children wade into puddles, tentatively at first. Then something happens. Their faces brighten and their eyes light up, and they splash with gleeful abandon. As this transformation occurs, Samantha lists the ways in which Forest School changes lives here.

There are the children labelled with behavioural problems before they have even started school who are calmed by the opportunity to run off some steam and give space to their eccentricities; the kids living in crowded flats who stop pushing and hitting after five sessions; the silent little girl for whom English is a second language who bursts into enthusiastic chatter when talking about the school; and then there is another group altogether.

Michael, for instance, was a four-year-old motor-mouth. On his first Forest School session, as his friends ran over bumpy, grassy terrain, he went silent, falling behind then stopping altogether. The teacher found him crying quietly and staring at his feet. She asked if his boots were hurting him. He shook his head and pointed at the ground. She asked if he wanted to hold her hand and he nodded. Patiently, she showed him how to lift his feet and walk over the uneven ground. Michael, you see, was so acclimatised to artificially flattened surfaces and concrete that he couldn't cope with naturally bumpy surfaces. It was the grassy ground itself that frightened him.

FACTS TO FIRE THE IMAGINATION

- It's down to grasses that cavemen evolved from hunter gatherers. They could farm them to harvest cereals to eat and graze cattle on them too.
- A garden lawn measuring 232m² (50ft by 50ft) has been claimed to produce enough oxygen to sustain a family of four.
- Today, most of the world's sugar comes from a grass called sugar cane.
- Grasses are the main food of tiny caterpillars, majestic deer and the Giant Panda, as well as many creatures in between.

TOOLKIT TO TAKE

Scissors
String
Jam jar
Paints
Brushes
White paper

IDEAS TO START WITH

BUILD A NEST

When in Rome, or in fact *out* in *spring*, do as the birds do at this time of year – build yourself a nest.

1 Go hunting for nest-building materials: grasses of different textures and lengths, as well as any twigs, leaves and mosses you come across.

2 Use the longer, sturdier varieties of grass to make loops of a few different sizes, tying the ends together to hold them in place.

3 Lay the loops inside each other. The biggest loop will be the top of your nest, the smaller ones forming the basic shape as it narrows towards the base.

4 Using these as your basic 'nest' shape, weave and prop shorter lengths of grass, twigs, leaves and whatever else you can get your hands on between the grass loops to make the nest stand up, bulk it out and give it structure and shape.

5 Find some 'eggs' to place in the nest (a few small, oval stones will do nicely. We've used everything from acorns to discarded beer-bottle tops).

Note Try using different materials and different construction methods to test them against each other.

HELP A BIRD BUILD A REAL HOME

Pity the poor Long-tailed Tit. It has to travel up to 1,126km (700 miles) to collect the lichen, moss, feathers, hair and spider's silk it needs to build a nest. It puts a weekend excursion to Ikea into perspective. So give it and other species a hand and do a spot of 'shopping' for them.

1 Go outside and hunt for nesting materials. Starlings use fresh green leaves from shrubs and moss raked from lawns, or fur, hair and wool. House Sparrows use straw and grasses, while House Martins, Song Thrushes and Blackbirds add mud to their nests.

2 When you have hunted down all your materials, collect them together and place them in or under a bush so that the birds can pilfer them easily and speedily.

MAKE A GRASS CROWN

The early Roman Empire went in for wreaths in a big way. Of those, the grass crown was the highest military decoration, reserved exclusively for soldiers whose actions saved a legion or entire army. A useful fact to entice a recalcitrant boy or resolutely un-princessy girl to follow in their lead.

1 Go out looking for some really good, sturdy long grass (reeds, for instance, are good here).

2 Collect the longest strands you can find.

3 Weave (or plait) several strands of grass together for strength, then loop them around your head and knot the ends together so that the crown fits.

4 Now decorate your crown. You can add flowers (their stems poked through the weave of the crown to secure them), or leaves or feathers… whatever best suits your heroic persona today.

ROLL DOWN A HILL

You don't need me to tell you how to do this, I know. Because, of course, the best way to do it is to forget all about instructions and the entire rule-bound world for one wild and wonderful, dizzying moment of hurtling downhill. If you want to know the fastest (and safest) way to make your way down a hill, however, here's how.

1 Locate a slope. The gradient, of course, depends on how much of a speed demon you are, but do remember to scout for rubbish, animal poo and electric fences at the bottom.

2 Get rid of anything that's going to encumber your descent: bags, bulky stuff in pockets – all these would slow your freewheeling joyride and may hurt you.

3 Lie down at a right angle to the slope. At any other angle you'll end up rolling across the hill.

4 Either keep your arms straight and stretched above your head, or cross them in front of your body.

5 THROW YOURSELF DOWN THE HILL.

6 Get up, and run back up the hill without stopping to give your head a chance to stop spinning.

7 DO IT AGAIN! AND AGAIN! AND AGAIN! (Don't be sick.)

Toddlers might like an adult positioned at the bottom of the hill to break their fall, as we did.

MAKE A GRASS BRASS BAND

The high-pitched whistle that's created with this trick is said to lure dangerous predators if done for long enough. These days, there are only a very few Coyotes, lynxes and Mountain Lions left in our own suburb of London but we don't dwell on that fact.

1   Find and pluck the perfect blade of grass. The ideal one will be at least as long as your thumb and good and wide.

2   Hold the blade of grass along the length of one thumb (its top at your finger tip, its end hanging down below the base of your thumb, pointing down towards your wrist).

3   Bring up the other thumb so that the blade is now sandwiched between your thumbs. Make sure the blade is flat and stretched quite tight.

4   Put your thumbs up to your lips and blow into the little space between, where the grass is visible.

5   If everything's in the right position, the grass should vibrate, creating a good, loud whistle.

CREATE A JAM-JAR GARDEN

1   Decide who is going to live in your jam-jar garden as this will determine the way you build and landscape it.

2   If it's for bugs you need to get practical. Stand the jam jar upright and create layers of different grasses, leaves, mud and moss with contrasting textures for the bugs to burrow through, explore and maybe have a munch on.

3   If it's for fairies you need a different sort of garden altogether   more ornamental than practical. Put a bit of mud at the bottom, then create a soft floor of grass cuttings and poke longer grasses and flowers through it, securing them in the mud below, to create a mini landscape of 'trees', 'shrubs' and 'meadows'. Pebbles and stones make good props, too. You can choose whether to lay your jar on its side or stand it upright.

4   Remember to quickly free any living visitors to your garden when you're done.

Note Plastic animals (including dinosaurs) also love a jam-jar garden. Remember that they will need lots of grass to graze on. Plastic cowboys, on the other hand, need long grass to take cover in during gunfights.

FIND A FOUR-LEAF CLOVER

Scientific American once researched the scientific probability of finding a lucky four-leaf clover. Its findings, very briefly, looked like this:

1 One in 10,000 clovers has four 'leaflets'.

2 A patch of clover generally has around 200 clovers per 60 cm² (9 in²) so...

3 You need to hunt through an area roughly the size of an office desk to take in the requisite 10,000.

4 The journal's 'expert clover hunters', supported by psychology studies, suggest that a 'quick-scan approach' works best. Rather than carefully inspecting each clover, scan a patch and wait for a plant to jump out at you (you might want to lightly brush the plants with your foot to separate them).

5 Your brain should automatically focus on anything you see that deviates from the norm.

6 Remember your spot. Four-leaf clovers are probably created by a genetic defect. Since many clover patches grow from just one plant, if you find one four-leaf clover in a patch, there might well be more. Note down the location of the patch or mark it with a stone so you can find it again.

7 Pick your lucky clover. You can press it (see page 76 – Blossom Pressing).

Toddlers will find the thrill of hunting for a lucky charm gripping enough, so with them just forget the science and the numbers.

WEAVE WITH GRASS

Nine hundred years ago the entire history of the Norman Conquest of England was woven into a masterpiece called the Bayeux Tapestry. It's 70 m long (230 ft) – a bit ambitious, perhaps, for an afternoon in the park. But you can create something equally beautiful (if a little smaller and more abstract).

1 Find four relatively straight sticks of a relatively even length.

2 Arrange the sticks into a square, their ends overlapping slightly, and secure the corners by tying lengths of string tightly around each. This is the frame of your loom.

3 Cut lengths of string a good bit longer than your loom. First, tie them in rows running horizontally across it, then in rows running vertically down it, weaving these under and over horizontal strings as you go. Now you have your loom.

4 Find long pieces of grass. Look for different textures and colours if you want to add variety and pattern to your weave.

5 Thread the grass pieces through your loom, winding under, then over the lengths of thread as you meet them.

6 When you have created a pattern you're happy with, you (or Grandma/fortunate friend or relative) can display your weave wherever desired. With a bit of re-imagination, the loom's twig frame can become a picture frame.

Toddlers will need wide spaces between the strings, so weaving the grass isn't too fiddly for them. They can try adding flowers for colour too.

Older children can bring the lengths of string closer together to make a tidier, more detailed weave. And they can try creating patterns and shapes with different textures and colours of grass.

EARTH

Do not trust it. It looks like the plainest, most banal material going. Yet one tablespoon of the stuff, scooped up from your back garden or the edge of the pavement, has more organisms within it than there are people on the globe. The very word contains such contradictory meanings, one monumental: Earth as in *the globe*; the other seemingly trivial: earth as in *a measly fleck of dirt*. It's the basis of everything: the ground beneath our feet, the thing that connects us to the planet and back through history to our ape ancestors… Or does it?

How much time do you actually spend with your bare toes wriggling in the soil? Do you, be honest now, find the idea a bit… distasteful? Our foraging forebearers had their (soon to be fossilised) feet on the ground in a very literal way. Thousands of years later, our own feet are more likely to be pounding pavements, defended from the indignity of dirt first by a thin covering of sock, then an inch of polyurethane shoe sole, under which might lie a thick layer of asphalt covering a layer of crushed stone compacted with a binder of bituminous material, perhaps a further 30 cm (12 in) of crushed aggregate base, then another 80 cm (30 cm) of 'sand sub-base' before you finally make it down to the earth, now, however, renamed as 'sub-grade'. It's quite a journey from shoe to soil.

Does all that make us less 'grounded', less 'connected' with or aware of the raw materials and reality of our environment? Probably. But when your house is 30 minutes from anywhere you might conceivably pull a carrot from the soil, but just three minutes from a supermarket shelf, and you engage in an instinctive slalom with litter on the journey to it, then dumping your prized shoe collection and staging a barefooted revolution looks a little reckless.

Instead, we choose to salvage our relationship with soil in a slightly less radical fashion. We make regular little visits to it, stick our fingers and feet in it, mould it, mash it, throw it, kick it,

giggle and squeal at it. Then we put our shoes back on to pound the pavements home. Where we wash it off.

FACTS TO FIRE THE IMAGINATION

- Earth is a mixture of materials, like completely rotted plant, ground-down rock and stones, and minerals.
- It takes a minimum of 500 years to form 2½ cm (1 in) of topsoil.
- Moles can dig up to 20 m (66 ft) of tunnel through the earth every day.
- Earthworms make good soil (or earth) by eating decaying matter and excreting much more fertile stuff, and by wriggling through the earth, mixing it as they go and bringing nutrients closer to the top.
- Ten per cent of the world's carbon dioxide emissions are stored in soil.
- Soil scientists, who study 'earth' for a living, typically define soil as the top 1.2 m (4 ft) of the earth's crust.

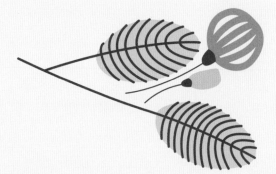

TOOLKIT TO TAKE

Magnifying glass
Trowel
Paper
Crayons
Jam jar and lid
Watch / stopwatch (or your
    mobile phone)

IDEAS TO START WITH

ANIMAL TRACK HUNT

Patiently hunting for animal tracks in the dirt can be an immensely satisfying way to spend an afternoon. If, however, you are short on patience but big on imagination, below I've also included a few curve-ball creatures for you to hunt....

Deer

Heron

Squirrel

Bigfoot

Dog

Badger

Duck

Fox

Frog

Blackbird

Rabbit

Cat

Gremlin

Sheep

Cow

Centaur

Dragon

Troll

PLAY SHADOW TAG

Sometimes it is not easy to persuade all the members of our family to leave the house. Sometimes certain members of the family go to great lengths to avoid walking the shortest of distances. Sometimes they suddenly fall gravely ill with mysterious illnesses, or are struck with terrible pains for which medical science knows no cure except television. These are the times we play shadow tag.

1   Find one or more opponents.

2   Decide who is going to be 'it' first. This person must then chase the shadows of the others, attempting to jump on one while the others weave and bob to avoid them. It is customary (but not obligatory) to squeal as well.

3   Once a person successfully jumps on someone's shadow, that person becomes 'it' and must try to jump on another shadow while everyone else runs away.

KEEPIE UPPIE (OF SORTS)

…well, the closest I get to it, anyway, as I have a clinical phobia of football. This game, though, I can get into. And since it can be played in a garden, playground or woodland, or even on a pavement if it is surrounded by low walls, I think it has the potential to be just as ubiquitous.

1   The aim of the game is to try and travel as far as you can without touching the earth, so pick a spot outside with lots of raised surfaces you might be able to walk along or clamber between.

2   Look for low walls, tree stumps, playground equipment and so on – can you all use them to cover space without your feet hitting the floor? Remember they need to be reliably strong and sturdy (if something breaks, you fall and hurt yourself, in which case you're going to lose in every sense).

3   Compete against each other – who can travel the furthest in the same environment before their feet have to touch the ground?

DRAW IN THE DIRT

Are you the Michelangelo of mud? The Degas of dirt? The Seurat of soil? If so…

1   Locate a good patch of earth, the bigger and clearer the better.

2   Find a stick.

3   Draw a masterpiece in the mud, using the stick.

MAKE A TREASURE MAP FOR A FRIEND

1 Select a location – it could be a local playground, park, garden or a bit of woodland.

2 Identify at least five landmarks within the location (for example a flower bed, a tree stump, a log or a bit of playground equipment). Leave two crossed sticks or a pile of stones as a marker in each location.

3 Now draw a map of the location, marking each landmark with a cross.

4 Give the map to your friend. Their challenge is to read the map and follow it to each of the landmarks, picking up each marker as they go to prove their success.

Toddlers will *probably* need a bit of assistance with the map drawing, but will be excellent at picking locations and using the map to hunt for markers.

Older children can make their maps more sophisticated, and might prefer the term 'orienteering' to 'treasure hunting'.

DO THE SQUEEZE TEST

All soils are classified in one of three ways. Clay soil is rich in nutrients but slow to drain. Sandy soil is quick draining but has trouble holding on to nutrients and moisture. Loam is considered the ideal soil as it holds moisture and nutrients but doesn't get soggy. You can use this super-simple squeeze test to find out what kind of soil you have.

1   Take a handful of moist (but not wet) soil and give it a firm squeeze.

2   Open your hand.

3   If the soil holds its shape and, when you give it a gentle poke, it crumbles, congratulations! You have the ideal soil – loam.

4   If it holds its shape and, when poked, sits stubbornly in your hand, you have clay soil.

5   If it falls apart as soon as you open your hand, you have sandy soil.

ANALYSE YOUR SOIL

This is one for the mini geologists and/or those who will enthusiastically embrace any enterprise that involves getting good and grubby.

1   Find some soil and put a handful or two in a jam jar.

2   Add twice as much water, put the lid on the jar and shake it well.

3   Leave for an hour, then peer closely at the contents.

4   If the water has settled, you should see different layers inside the jar. Sunk to the very bottom you'll find any pebbles plus a layer that's made up of the sand that was inside the mud. Next up is a layer of silt. On top of that you'll see the water, turned murky as the organic materials from the soil (rotting plants, mostly) have dissolved into it. Floating at the very top will be the organic material that was in the soil but which hasn't yet fully rotted.

Older children can also learn the reason sand sinks to the bottom, because sand particles are the biggest and heaviest. Silt particles are small and lighter, so they sit on top.

CHARM AN EARTHWORM FROM THE GROUND

Earthworm charming – in essence, thumping on the ground to lure worms to the surface by vibration – is quite literally a serious business, since in North America it exists as a profession called 'grunting'. Pro 'grunters' sell their charmed worms to bait shops for fishing with. In Britain, sadly, it is viewed merely as sport. At the Woodhall Worm Charming Festival, held in Lincolnshire, entrants are given 30 minutes to lure as many worms from the ground as they can by whatever means possible. Only digging and the pouring of water are banned.

1 After some rain, gather your friends and find an area of damp soil on which to charm your worms.

2 Gather materials with which to try thumping the ground – rocks, sticks, branches, your feet and a trowel are all fair game.

3 Set your watch. Thirty minutes might be ambitious, so knock off a zero and go for three minutes.

4 Shout 'On your marks, get set, go!' and start your various charming techniques.

5 Keep your eyes peeled to see what comes wriggling up through the ground. The winner is the person who has charmed the most (or any!) worms to the surface when the time is up.

TRY PARKOUR

Is it a bird? Is it a plane? No, it's us pounding around and scraping our shins again. If your neighbourhood, like ours, has more sidewalk than soil then at least there's parkour. The sport otherwise known as 'free running' has made pavements peerlessly cool and turned hemmed in streets into playgrounds of endless possibility. It seems ironic that this – the most urban of sports – should bring people closest to the freedoms of a creature in the wild.

Vaulting off the city architecture, you're as free as a bird, leaping like a Leopard, swooping like a seagull, dodging like a deer… or, in our case, possibly more like a Dachshund. Parkour, it turns out, is actually quite tricky. Practising in our local playground, we often come home covered in grazes more than in glory. But here are some basic moves you can, with a lot of practice and caution, perfect and impress with.

Adults, when your family is ready to try parkour, make sure you start small and continually assess your kids' capabilities.

1 Perfect your jump

Find a bench or low wall, and practise jumping safely and comfortably to the ground. First jump with both feet, landing with them together, then practise with one foot leading you. Alternate your leading foot until you get the hang of it.

Once older children have tried a 'leading foot jump', practise taking a running start and jumping while moving. Then they can practise from a (slightly!) greater height.

2 Learn to leap over things (without bumping them, or stopping)

Find an object – not too intimidating to start with – to jump over. At first, the height of a few bricks will do fine. Take a little run up to it and – leading with one foot and lifting both legs to clear it – jump over it. When you can do this without slowing down or touching the object, and carry on running after landing, then find a slightly bigger obstacle to jump over.

3 Perfect your vault

You'll need a long and short object to perfect this – a low wall to start with. Place both hands on the wall's surface and use them to propel your body horizontally over it, with your legs flung out to the right. As you lift over your body, pick up your right hand first, and continue to support and propel yourself with the left one until your feet are swinging down to the ground. Got it? Now try a run-up to the wall…

4 Balance better

Balance, we've learnt in a wobbly fashion, is key to parkour. You can practise it by walking along the short walls that border pavements, standing on one foot wherever you are or using low playground equipment.

Older children There are lots of guides and videos online if kids want to learn other moves. Learning to roll properly after landing is a good one for them to tackle next. Just encourage them to take it slowly and responsibly.

RIVERS, STREAMS AND PONDS

When I think about the 'perfect childhood', it's rivers and streams that always come to mind.

The childhood of dreams is spent beside the water, racing and skipping along its banks. Chasing butterflies or learning fly fishing with a home-made rod. Listening to the whispers of a cascade, tantalising you with adventure just out of view. Watching dragonflies dart over the long grass and streaks of salmon leaping upstream. Skimming stones and scraping knees and dusting them off and lighting fires (on which you will later, of course, eat the fish you have caught while huddled under blankets and singing folk songs to the accompaniment of a bashed-up guitar that has materialised from the ether).

The 'perfect childhood' and its conscience-pricking counterpart 'the river of dreams' are so called for a reason: that's the only place they exist. I can't find the river on any road map because it's not real. Not really. Not unless you are an *extremely* lucky person living in an *extremely* lovely location. Otherwise, you have to settle for approximations. These do exist and some of them are even pretty close relations of the dream. Here are some hard-learned facts about them:

1 They will be just 30 minutes away according to Google Maps' calculations, but will nevertheless always take you an hour and 45 minutes because of a) a hideous pile-up on the motorway, b) weekend roadworks, c) someone's incomprehensible yet inherent inability to read a simple map.
2 When you get there, someone will have a) had a horrible row in the car, b) developed hay fever, c) had a sleep in the car, rendering them hell-bent on

remaining grumpy for the next 20 minutes, (e) forgotten a wellington boot.

3 The 'almost river of dreams' proves, in reality a) to be really quite close to the gathering point of the local branch of the Hells Angels, b) to sit just off a major arterial road, c) to have dried to a slightly less impressive trickle approximately ten years ago (just after, it turns out, the map was last printed).

4 You will have fun anyway – as soon as you adjust to this reality. Real rivers are, in fact, much more interesting than their imagined counterparts because a) they have real people bringing them to life (your people, the ones who have occasional tantrums and read maps upside down), b) moustached muscle men on motorbikes make fascinating zoological specimens to spy on (I mean 'study') from afar, c) all these distractions disappear as soon as you start splashing and dashing around. Oh, and d) one welly is plenty as long as you have a plastic bag and some gaffer tape in the car.

- In the last century 70 per cent of the UK's ponds have disappeared.
- Insects called pond skaters can literally walk on water. They use surface tension and the little hairs on their feet to repel water and skate across the tops of ponds.
- The longest river in the world is the River Nile which is 6,650 km (4,132 miles) long.
- If you added them together, all the world's rivers still only make up roughly 0.0002 per cent of the Earth's water.
- Still, more than 65 per cent of our drinking water comes from rivers and streams.

TOOLKIT TO TAKE

Magnifying glass
Trowel
Jam jar
String
Foil takeaway container
Scissors
Towel

IDEAS TO START WITH

SKIM A STONE

The record for stone skimming is held by an American called Russell Byers, who managed to bounce (or 'skim') a stone 51 times across a body of water. Meanwhile, skimming 'experts' are apparently divided as to the optimal stone for skimming, some championing the smooth ones, others defending pitted surfaces (which apparently reduce water drag). On the subject of this global controversy I remain neutral – the Switzerland of stone skimming. But here, very basically, is how to do it:

1 Find a flat stone – as thin and light as possible and roughly the size of your palm.

2 Crouch down as low as you can to the water.

3 Hold the stone between your thumb and forefinger.

4 Bring your arm back, then send the stone across the water from just above ankle height. Use as much force as you can and throw the stone as horizontally as possible.

5 As you throw the stone, spin it with a flick of your wrist when you release it.

6 Count how many bounces the stone makes before disappearing.

MAKE POOH STICKS

A classic, this...

1 Find a river or stream with a bridge over it.

2 Take a friend (or friends) to search for sticks.

3 Stand on one side of the bridge and, on the count of three, drop your sticks simultaneously into the water.

4 Run to the other side of the bridge, and see whose stick emerges first.

SAIL A BOAT

A couple of years ago we helped to start a local Woodcraft Folk group with some other families who like to get outdoors. Like a secular Scouts, it's less hippy than it sounds. This activity was one of the first things we did together, and is still one of the most popular.

1 Collect some sticks, as straight as you can find.

2 Break or cut the sticks into roughly matching lengths.

3 Line up the sticks next to each other, like a rectangle-shaped barcode.

4 Now bind the sticks tightly together with string (weaving it between them and knotting tightly).

5 Lay a couple of new sticks at right angles across this surface – one at the top and one at the bottom – to strengthen the 'raft'.

6 Tie these to the structure with string.

7 Ram a feather or a piece of bark between two sticks at the front of the raft so that it stands straight up and makes a sail.

8 Now sail or race your boats. Blow them along with your own puff if you're at a pond, or let them drift downstream if you have flowing water at your disposal.

Toddlers will need help with this which, here, comes in the form of fathers who (anecdotal research suggests) take an average of 31.4 seconds to become engrossed to the point of complete, competitive obsession.

GO MUDLARKING

Is there any better word than mudlarking? Georgian in origin, the term means 'wandering along a river's shoreline, scavenging anything shiny, from ancient bullion to rusty Coke cans (that's the modern version, at least...). Once a way for London's poor to find saleable trinkets fallen from passing boats, it's now a brilliant diversion for families.

1   Head down to the bank of a river.

2   Walk up and down alongside the river's edge, hunting for bits of pottery, buttons, tools and even bones.

3   Collect your finds and create stories around their origins and how they ended up washed up on a riverbank.

Note Remember to check tide tables, beware of sharp and rusty things, and wash your hands after mudlarking.

JAM-JAR FISHING

1   Cut a decent length of string (as tall as you, roughly).

2   Loop one end of the string tightly around the neck of a jam jar and tie it on.

3   Hold the string and give the jar a good shake to make sure it doesn't fall off.

4   If you are on a soft bank of a deep river, hurl the jam jar out as far as you can (making VERY SURE you are holding onto the other end of the string else all will be lost). If you are by a rocky, shallow stretch of water, lower the jar in gently.

5   Pull the jar back to you, and examine the contents. 1 point for traces of muck; 2 points for bits of plant life; 3 points for stones; 4 points for litter; 5 points for tiny fish or other pond life. Return any living organisms to the river once you have counted them.

POND DIPPING

This is much the same method as that used for jam-jar fishing, only it's done in still water. It's good, too, to have a foil takeaway container beside you, so you can tip the contents of the jam jar into it and examine your finds more closely with a magnifying glass. Always return living things to the pond after you've finished looking at them.

What you might see while you're at the pond

Frog spawn

Snail

Damselfly

Dragonfly

Frog

Water Boatman

Whirligig Beetle

Tadpole

Pond Skater

Newt

PREDICT THE AGE OF A TADPOLE

- At 10 days after hatching: tadpoles start to swim around and eat algae.
- At 6 weeks: they grow short back legs.
- At 9 weeks: their 'arms' start to develop.
- At 12 weeks: their tails shrink to short stumps.

SINKERS AND FLOATERS

I promised my family that I wouldn't include embarrassing details about them in this book. So. Hypothetically, if you have a child who finds the word floater so extraordinarily hilarious that its use, in any situation, results in paroxysms of helpless snorting, weeping, convulsing and shuddering… And if, hypothetically, you have a husband who, though technically well advanced into middle age, suffers from the same debility, then you might send them off to do this together – between fits of howling – while you have an extremely well-earned rest.

1 Find a pond or deep puddle. Flowing water isn't as good but will do if needs be.

2 Each person collects as many different materials of varying shapes and weights as they can: stones, leaves, twigs, grass, flowers… You cannot have two of the same object – each one must be different in some way.

3 The winner is the person with the most 'floaters' when their objects are dropped into the water, so…

4 When you have your collections, stand next to the patch of water and take it in turns to drop any object into it.

5 If it sinks, bellow, 'SINKER!'

6 If it floats, roar, 'FLOATER!' Then double over laughing, as if physically assaulted by your own wit.

Older children If they can get past the sniggering, this is actually a pretty good way of exploring the science of density: sinkers sink because they are more dense than floaters.

SWIM

Search the Outdoor Swimming Society's website and you'll find a plethora of relatively safe wild swimming spots, wherever you are. To make them kid-friendly, here are some suggestions.

1 Select somewhere with easy access, like a gently sloping bank or beach.

2 Get an adult to check that it isn't too deep, and there aren't any obstructions, further in.

3 Wear something on your feet: jelly shoes, wetsuit boots, old trainers... They'll help you explore without worry.

4 MOVE ABOUT MANICALLY! It will keep you warm.

5 Stick close to the bank until you get used to the cold water, and always stay close to your group.

6 Have towels ready to hop into as soon as the shivers set in, and a thermos of something hot, too.

Important note Wild swimming is the best, but you really do need to be extremely careful. Never swim anywhere you're not absolutely certain is 100 per cent safe.

GO AMPHIBIAN (AND WATER MONSTER) HUNTING

Amphibians, *of course*, are animals that live both in water and on land, although they all start their lives in water, and with gills and tails. Frogs, for example, are amphibians, and they were celebrated by the ancient Egyptians as symbols of life and fertility. In medieval Europe, however, frogs were seen as satanic, so whatever your degree of squeamishness you can now justify it with a historical context.

Take a magnifying glass down to a pond and see if you can spot any of these:

Kelpie

Tadpoles

Newt

Frog

Kappa

Frog spawn

Loch Ness monster

Grindylow

Toad spawn

Toad

CATCH A FISH (BY SURPRISE)

1 Wearing wellies, wade a little way into a stream and stand very, veeeeeeery still.

2 Do any little fish approach? How close will they come before you startle them off?

TRY THE WATERFALL 'YOGA' POSITION

1 Stand with your feet hip-distance apart and breathe deeply.

2 Stretch your arms straight up above your head.

3 Gently bend back ever so slightly, opening up your chest, and imagine a waterfall flowing off the tips of your fingers and onto the ground beneath them.

Note I'm no yogi, so these aren't professional instructions. Find a qualified instructor if you want to explore yoga properly.

DANDELIONS AND DAISIES

Weeds, weeds, wonderful weeds. Daises and dandelions are so hardy that it's said they grow everywhere on Earth except Antarctica. Their tenacious spirits might make them sworn enemies of fathers-in-law and their prized lawns across the land, but it's also turned them into the playthings of kids around the world and throughout history, since they can be picked in meadows and fields, between pavement slabs and in parking lots.

On dull Sundays, when time itself bloats and stretches out drowsily like the adults after their lunch; during interminable, dust-veiled visits to great aunts; and in school holidays when the neighbourhood is a ghost town and everyone else in the world has gone to the seaside, there will always be dandelions.

It's all a matter of perspective. Personally, having no prize lawn but two wild kids to entertain, I'm a fan. And so, it turns out, is Kelly Broadfield, resident warden at Dodford Children's Holiday Farm. 'We basically cultivate weeds on purpose,' she says, looking out over the gardens of the big, red brick house where she lives and works. In 1951, it opened its doors to deprived inner-city families that needed a respite from their bomb-shattered, smog-choked post-war neighbourhoods.

Today, it still offers holidays of up to a week to inner-city school groups and struggling families that need a break. Most come from the nearby city of Birmingham, referred by social workers, GPs and community workers. If kids come with their parents, it's not uncommon for neither generation to have never seen a farm animal in the flesh before.

'The children may have seen one in a book,' says Kelly. 'Parents sometimes tentatively approach one of our larger, male sheep, then admit, "I've never been this close to a sheep before. It *is* a sheep, isn't it?"'

Often the children arrive with special needs or behavioural problems. But, Kelly says, it's commonly the parents who struggle to adjust to life on the farm. 'They've been raised without contact with nature, too. The younger kids leap out of the car, see the animals and are off. For some of the adults, though, the darkness and silence scares them. While they might need the feel-good factor of spending time outdoors with the animals just as much as the kids, it's usually them who crack, two days in, and say they need to take the family home.'

So weeds have become a key weapon in Kelly's charm offensive. Each day she and the staff lead a gaggle of kids and adults outside. They lend them wellies and waterproofs and, in spring, the kids carry buckets to gather up dandelion leaves. When they have enough, they feed them to the guinea pigs and rabbits, and move on to the pigs, sheep and donkeys, too.

'It has such a therapeutic effect on them,' says Kelly, 'even the most severely autistic kids. After a couple of days, their parents and teachers say how much better they are acting, how much more settled they are, how much better they are sleeping and eating. Because nature doesn't judge you on your unusual behaviour or your wheelchair. And neither do animals. As long as you bring the dandelion leaves they are happy!'

FACTS TO FIRE THE IMAGINATION

- The English common name dandelion comes from the French *dent de lion*, meaning tooth of the lion. Rather rudely dandelions are also known in French as *pissenlit*, or pee the bed, because dandelion has traditionally been used as a diuretic.

- A dandelion clock is said to contain a hundred or more seeds. Each seed has its own parachute to help it travel in the wind.
- Daisies have traditional been used as a medicine to treat colds and flu and even relieve indigestion.
- It's thought that the word 'daisy' comes from 'day's eye', because of the way its petals open at dawn and close at dusk.

TOOLKIT TO TAKE

Jam jar
Paper
Brush
PVA glue
Crayons
Paints
Needle and thread
Scissors

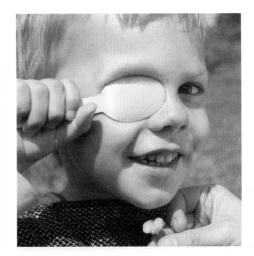

IDEAS TO START WITH

MAKE DANDELION CHAINS

We first saw these being made by three girls, sitting on a dusty kerb, during a 'Playing Out' session. In 2009, a group of neighbours in Bristol decided to close their road to traffic for a few hours, so children could play. It snowballed and today streets all over the country hold their own regular 'Playing Out' sessions. For a few hours, scooters and bikes replace cars. Roller-skates weave around hopscotch players and chalk-wielding street artists. This time, as we stood wide-eyed amid the mini-revolution, there were also dandelion chains – just like old-fashioned daisy chains but bigger and brasher. We liked the look of it, tried it and loved it ourselves.

1 Gather up some dandelions, keeping good, long stems attached to them.
2 Use your thumbnail to pierce a hole in the stem of your first dandelion.
3 Thread the stem of your second dandelion all the way through the hole, stopping at the flower.
4 Now make a hole in the stem of the second dandelion and thread a third through that.
5 Make a hole in the third dandelion, and continue until you have enough for a bracelet, crown or even belt.
6 Thread the stem of the last dandelion through a small slit at the top of the first to complete the circle.

CURL DANDELION STEMS

1 Use your thumbnail or a knife to separate a dandelion stem into several long strands.
2 Fill a jam jar with some water and drop the stem sections into the water.
3 Watch the stems curl up – it happens almost immediately.
4 Use the curled stems for anything from collages to (pretend) cooking (they make great 'noodles' in a mud soup).

Older children This is, of course, an exercise in osmosis, if you want to explore the science behind it.

MAKE DANDELION CLOCKS

Some people claim that the number of seeds remaining once you've blown the powder-puff top off a dandelion clock represents the number of years you have left to live. This seeming a little morbid for a four-year-old (a bit of a dampener on playtime), we tend to go for the more common tradition: using it to tell the time.

1 Find a dandelion whose flower has matured into a spherical seed head, or clock (known as a blowball in North America).

2 Blow hard.

3 Count your puffs like this: '1 o'clock... 2 o'clock... 3 o'clock...', until all the seeds are gone. Whatever 'o'clock' you reach with your last puff is the time.

CREATE DANDELION-CLOCK PICTURES

When we're out of puff, or want to give the house a slightly longer break from the kids' campaign of pillaging and destruction, we move on to one of the following activities.

1 Gather some dandelion clocks.

2 Have a think about what pictures you can make with their fluffy seeds. Clouds? Furry animals?

3 Take out some paper, and use a brush to paint a shape in glue.

4 Now blow your dandelion over the paper, so that it sticks to the glue.

5 Give the paper a little shake, and voila!

6 You can add details to the rest of the picture in crayon or paint.

OR... PAINT WITH A DANDELION FLOWER

Dunk the heads of your dandelion flowers into paint, and brush, twist, blob and rub them into the paper, making different patterns as you go.

Toddlers A big, muddy brown mess might be more their style.

Older children can experiment with different styles: little pointellist prints, impressionist smudges, abstract impressionist dribbles and smears...

OR... MAKE DANDELION INVISIBLE INK

1 Cut off the stem from one of your dandelions at a 45-degree angle, so that it looks like the nib of a fountain pen.

2 If you squint, you'll see a whitish sap inside.

3 Draw or write with it on paper. You'll need to press firmly, and to regularly replace your dandelion pen with a newly cut stem.

4 Your message or picture will look pretty much invisible at first, but leave it to dry and you'll see it emerge.

DECORATE YOURSELF WITH DAISIES

1. Make daisy-chain necklaces, bracelets, head-dresses and rings (see Dandelion Chains on page 47 for instructions).

2. Weave long chains through belt hoops on trousers.

3. Tuck single stems behind your ears.

4. Thread stems through buttonholes on shirts to decorate them, or cufflink holes to decorate work-weary fathers.

5. Crown yourself the Daisy King or Queen.

6. Make earrings by piercing the green underside of the flower (where the stem begins) with a needle and thread, before removing the needle and tying the thread in a loop that's large enough to fit over your ear with the flower hanging down. Tada!

MAKE FAIRY FOOD

Fairies have a rich and varied diet. Depending on the places we've been and the seasons we've encountered, we have persuaded them to eat everything from grass cuttings to mouldy bark (and, on one desperate occasion, beer-bottle tops). They are, basically, greedy and indiscriminate. Scavenge for stuff outdoors, chop it into tiny pieces and gather it into a small vessel of any sort, and they will eat it. That said, daisy petals are a fairy delicacy. Though greedy, they will eat only whole petals, very carefully removed without tearing them… It's a quirk of theirs.

1. Gather together some daisies.

2. Remove the petals from the flowers, being *extremely* careful not to tear them.

3. Put the petals in something bowl shaped: a shell, an acorn cap or even a leaf will do.

4. Find a quiet, sheltered spot to leave the bowl – the base of a tree, a hole in a trunk… that kind of thing.

5. Do not expect to see the fairies come to eat it. They are notoriously private creatures and won't arrive until you disappear from view (another quirk).

EAT THEM

'Honestly, you can,
I promise – they are
nutritious and delicious.
YOU'LL LOVE THEM!!!!
JUST TRY ONE...' Repeat
ad infinitum.

1 Collect dandelions.

2 Remove the petals and wash them, carefully.

3 Scatter the petals over a salad to make it beautifully
   colourful, and eat this (or, more probably, watch your parents
   do so).

AIR

And so it was that we found ourselves, after a whole spring of small outdoor adventures, in a car creaking under the weight of nappies, wipe-down surfaces and waterproof kit, about to undertake something momentous: a family and friends camping trip.

The great poet Walt Whitman thought he'd discovered what he called *'the secret of making the best persons, it is to grow in the open air and to eat and sleep with the earth'*. He obviously hadn't tried erecting a new tent in the drizzling dusk with one screaming child playing buckaroo on his back and another clinging to his leg in the throes of cold turkey from cartoons.

The stove we had borrowed stubbornly refused to light, the blow-up bed had a hole the size of the baby's fist in its side, and we had somehow managed to underestimate just how 'fresh' fresh air gets in during the depths of the night, when you have only a thin flap of tent between you and it, and some children have invaded your duvet before commando-rolling away with it. It was, dear reader, a long, long night.

Then, at around 4.30 a.m., cold, cramped and cowering from the first light that was dribbling like weak tea through the canvas walls, something amazing happened. It started with a lone, questioning voice. Then came a rakish responding one. Soon it was as if the chorus line of every Broadway show had crowded onto a single stage, a little drunk, to give full-pelted voice to all their different songs at once.

Apparently, the dawn chorus only lasts for three months of the year, reaching its peak at exactly the time we'd picked to pitch our tent, in mid spring when food becomes more plentiful, the breeding season begins and local birds are joined by other species that drop at the end of their migration.

Not that I knew this at the time. Then, all I could think was how on earth our cheap double glazing had insulated us from this cacophony at home for all these years. It was so loud that I worried it would wake the kids. Sure enough, 'What is that?' came a small, muffled voice from below a pilfered sleeping bag. 'I think it's the dawn chorus,' an adult replied. 'I like the dawnosaurus,' said the voice.

FACTS TO FIRE THE IMAGINATION

- Air is a mixture of different gases that cover the entire Earth in a layer called 'the atmosphere'.
- Almost every single animal and plant on the planet needs air to survive.
- Air protects us by absorbing harmful rays from the sun and reducing extremes of temperature.
- Air is made up of roughly 78 per cent nitrogen, 21 per cent oxygen and smaller amounts of argon, hydrogen, carbon dioxide and others.

TOOLKIT TO TAKE

Crayons
String
Scissors
Magnifying glass
Jam jar
Paper
Your ears
Your eyes
Your nose

IDEAS TO START WITH

CLOUD SPOTTING

. . . .

We do this *a lot* – on car journeys, standing in queues, waiting for food to cook… You can do it in a sweeping valley or on a soaring high-rise building, *anywhere* as long as you can see the sky.

1 Look up.

2 What shapes are the clouds making? Can you see a dragon? Or a car? A castle?

3 If you're in a group, take turns to spot things and point them out. If you're on your own, just let it roll – the only limitation is your imagination.

ADVANCED CLOUD SPOTTING

. . . .

You can do a more grown-up version, if you want, and see if you can identify the official cloud type above you. The guide on the opposite page will help you know what you're looking for.

GET UP FOR THE DAWN CHORUS

I'll give it to you straight: 4.30 a.m. is early. It's an ungodly hour at which to heave a heavy lump of bed-hair and creased pyjamas from their bed and carry them, writhing and moaning, to the local park. If you are going to attempt this, you should stick like glue to the following guidelines.

1 Consider your location. I'm all for ambition, but realism is your watchword here. You don't need to be somewhere remote to hear it. The leafy areas of a city will get a good chorus, too, so a balcony or garden – somewhere close to home and bed – might be preferable to a distant field.

2 Check that the place you've chosen is accessible at 4.30 a.m. (you do *not* want to arrive at the park gates to f ind them padlocked).

3 Verify the time at which the sun will rise: the dawn chorus peaks between half an hour *before* and half an hour *after* sunrise. You don't want to miss it.

4 Make a big flask of hot chocolate and a generous pile of something warm and sweet to eat (we like hot, buttered, sticky malt loaf, wrapped in lots of tin foil).

5 Remember warm clothes. VERY warm ones.

6 Wake your companions in good time.

7 Find a comfortable spot to wait in, then open your hot chocolate and snacks immediately.

8 Listen…

Cirrus

Cirrocumulus

High level
above 6,000 m

Cirrostratus

Altocumulus

Mid level
2,000 – 6,000 m

Altostratus

Stratocumulus

Nimbostratus

Cumulus

Low level
0 – 2,000 m

Stratus

Cumulonimbus

HOW MANY DIFFERENT KINDS OF BIRDSONG CAN YOU HEAR?

If you feel you can't burden friends and family with your own mood at 4.30 a.m., then I sympathise. Here's a softer option for you and (who am I kidding?) me.

1 Leave the house at a more civilised time of day.

2 Stand somewhere with a decent smattering of trees.

3 Open your ears.

4 Try to discern and count the different types of birdsong you can hear.

Older children can find audio guides to birdsong on the RSPB's website.

SPOTTING BIRDS

There are no real 'rules' to this game. If you're old enough to remember the *Pink Panther* films, it might help to think of your role akin to that of Cato, the manservant employed by Clouseau to jump out and attack him at any given moment in order to keep him on his toes.

1 The game is *always* on.

2 Keep your eyes and ears open wherever you go.

3 You've won if you are able to shout 'LONG-TAILED TIT!' with a large enough element of surprise that someone drops their shopping.

TRY THE AEROPLANE 'YOGA' MOVE

This is really quite difficult to balance in, so it's best attempted slowly, with caution and on a soft surface.

1 Stand up straight, with your feet hips-width apart and your arms by your sides.

2 As you breathe out, stretch out your arms to either side, at shoulder height.

3 Breathe in and bend forwards at the hips.

4 Find a spot on the horizon to focus on – this will help you balance. Breathe out.

5 Breathe in slowly and lift one leg off the floor so that it is stretches out directly behind you (don't push yourself, though!).

6 Breathe out and return your foot to the floor. Now try the same again, using the other leg.

SPRING SMELLS AND SOUNDS

Lots of creatures – hedgehogs, rabbits, mice and badgers, to name just a few – rely heavily on their sense of smell. My own family has a genetic advantage that allows us to identify and hunt down a fish-and-chip shop from extreme distances. Otherwise, our sense of smell is pretty shabby in comparison to that of most woodland animals. Here's how to sharpen your senses.

1 Head outdoors. Woodland is good, but anywhere in the open will do.

2 How many sounds and smells of spring can you identify?

3 Start at ground level – are there animals rustling or shuffling? Can you smell freshly cut grass?

4 Then move up to the shrubs and flowers – more rustling? Birds being startled from branches? Bees buzzing? Flowers fragrant?

5 Now higher, to the branches of trees and the sky – can you hear birdsong, or insects? Catch the scents carried on the breeze?

Note You can make this a competition against friends, if you want. The winner is the one who notices the most sounds and smells, but beware cheats: make sure everyone points their finds out as they go.

GIVE OUTDOOR MEDITATION A GO

In order to thoroughly road test this book, I have tried this activity on my four year old. I am therefore fully equipped to tell you that it is better suited to older children who do not need to be bribed with fudge to sit still for more than 15 seconds. It does, however, work as well for adults as for these more mature children, if you can give your four-year-old the slip for a few minutes.

1 Find a spot to sit in outdoors. It should be somewhere comfortable and quiet, as far away from the noise of traffic and people as is practically possible.

2 Cross your legs and rest your hands on your knees.

3 Breathe in slowly for ten counts.

4 Breathe out slowly for ten counts.

5 Open your mind to the sounds around you and listen to them with no fixed purpose for a minute or so, bringing your mind back to the sound of your environment if it wanders elsewhere.

6 Now try to focus on one sound at a time – a bird, perhaps, or the wind – so that the other noises fade into the background. Give each sound a minute or two, before moving on to the next.

7 When you are ready, open your eyes slowly and look up at the sky, noticing the patterns made by clouds and even aircraft.

8 Lower your eyes slightly, and take in the leaves of any trees and their movements in the breeze.

9 Finally, lower your gaze so that you are looking straight ahead of you, breathe in and notice the scents and smells of your environment. Try to appreciate the quiet workings of the natural world, which are going on all around us as we race about with our busy lives.

GO CAMPING

You'll have to pretend I didn't suggest this one, since I suppose it calls for quite a few things that aren't in our toolkit. But, but, but… I couldn't let spring pass without a nod to camping.

I'm not suggesting anything fancy. Fling a blanket over a couple of chairs on a balcony, spread a sheet over a garden table, or borrow a basic tent and pitch it anywhere convenient – even if it's only for a few hours in the middle of the afternoon, just out of sight of a motorway.

Take snacks and a flask. Peer out at the world from behind your canvas/sheet/blanket. There's something about this that can't be beaten – even if you're the kind of person for whom the bit where you go home to a warm shower and clean sheets is the most thrilling of all.

MAKE A RAINBOW OF YOUR OWN

Put some water in a jam jar and take it into the sunshine or, if you're indoors, place it near a window. Lay a piece of white paper in direct sunlight and hold your jar above it, but close to it. Slowly change the position and tilt of the jar, watching the effect it has on the paper. When you get the right spot and angle, the sunlight will pass through the water, bending (or 'refracting') and thus projecting a tiny rainbow onto your piece of paper.

Note Pick a time when the sun is strong and high in the sky.

INSECTS

'What's the difference between a bug and an insect?' This question was asked over breakfast one morning, and three generations of hand – from a buttery four-year-old fist to an age-spotted seventy-year-old one – halted on their journeys to their mouths, leaving their toast suspended thoughtfully in the air.

'It's the same thing, one's slang, one's, erm, official.' 'Insects have wings, bugs live under logs.' 'Yeah, but spiders are insects, right?' – communal grunts of approval – 'But spiders don't have wings...'

So, of course, I got on Google. 'All insects belong to the phylum arthropoda,' I preached across the pots of jam. 'Arthropod actually means "jointed leg" so any mini-beast with those falls into that category, including all insects, spiders, ticks, centipedes... you name it. But the class insect is then separated into lots of orders. Dragonflies are in one. Beetles in another, and bugs in yet another. Bugs are defined by the fact that, rather than having mouths as we understand them, their mouth-parts are all designed for piercing and sucking the sap from plants.'

Four sets of eyes were glued to mine. Four mouths made different noises, ranging from 'WOW!' to 'eurgghhhhh...'

But did it matter that we hadn't known the proper classifications? That words like hemiptera, stylet, phylum and arthropod were still making us stutter, mutter and splutter our crumbs rather than tripping confidently from our tongues?

In a Guardian article by Liu Xinyan, I read that a Chinese charity called Friends of Nature has been attempting to reconnect the country's urban children to nature, in cities where that contact has been so completely severed, they say, that both adults and children can be sent into screams of panic at the sight of an ant. What they have learnt, over the years, is this: while it's good for kids to know the names of various species, a great deal more is gained if they can recognise their beauty. What's most valuable of all, is if – in some loose, undefined way that cannot be pinned down with a Latin categorisation – they can sense and appreciate the natural cycle that connects a beautiful, unknown flower to their own lives.

Empowered to connect with nature casually and organically, away from the classroom and its urge to quantify value and measure results, some of the children the charity worked with grew more focused, others more imaginative, some more peaceful, others braver. Most experienced each of these qualities in different moments.

So. FACTS! KNOW YOUR LIMITS! A well-chosen bit of knowledge is invaluable when it acts as a spark to ignite the imagination. Did you know, for instance, that insects represent somewhere between 80 and 90 per cent of all life forms found on Earth? NINETY! And according to the nature guru David Attenborough, 'If we and the rest of the back-boned animals were to disappear overnight, the rest of the world would get on pretty well. But if the invertebrates were to disappear, the world's ecosystem would collapse.'

Remember, though, that the most important thing is to get bogged down in the real mud, not the facts. We might not have known the precise terms, but bugs, insects, creepy crawlies and mini-beasts were our first guides into the natural world. When puddles left the kids pouting, on the occasions when trees were trumped by telly you could bet your right hand and life savings on a damp log. Upturn it and reveal a world of blind, busily burrowing bugs beneath it, and we would all be spellbound in seconds.

FACTS TO FIRE THE IMAGINATION

- Instead of a nose, ants use their antennae to smell with and worms breathe through their skins.
- Centipedes don't really have 100 legs – British species have anywhere between 15 and 101 pairs, and it's always an odd number of pairs. They do, however, have poisonous jaws for capturing their prey.
- Shield bugs are sometimes called 'stink bugs' because they create a terrible stench if threatened.
- It's thought that snails can lift up to 10 times their own body weight. Ants, however, are said to be even tougher, heaving up to 50 times their own weight.

TOOLKIT TO TAKE

Magnifying glass
Jam jar
White sheet
Trowel
Plastic cup
Brush
Paper
Paints
Foil takeaway container
Sellotape
Plastic bottle
Scissors
Skewer
String

IDEAS TO START WITH

GO ON A HABITAT HUNT

This was our first, favourite and possibly simplest thing to do in nature.

1. Go out habitat hunting. We're looking for damp, dark places so...

2. Explore the undersides of logs and rocks, sift through soil, beneath leaf piles, in the dark recesses beneath plants and so on.

3. Closer to home, check window frames and sills, guttering and drainpipes, and the cracks between paving stones.

4. Turn over your habitat gently or poke around in it very carefully.

5. What minibeasts can you find sheltering there? Look out for centipedes, woodlice and spiders.

6. Use a brush to lift the creatures gently into a plastic cup or jam jar.

7. Inspect them with a magnifying glass. What colours are they? How many legs does each one have? Do they have wings? What do you think they eat?

8. Put the wee beasties back, gently, when you're done and return their home to the way it was when you found it.

Older children might want to try to identify and classify the insects.

SHAKE DOWN A TREE (GENTLY, NOW)

1. Find a tree or a bush.

2. Lay a white sheet on the ground below it, or hold it under its branches.

3. Give a branch a gentle shake over the sheet.

4. What bugs have fallen from the branches they were perched on? Watch out for shield bugs, spiders and ladybirds.

5. When you've thoroughly examined the bugs, gently shake them from the sheet into the grass and move on to a different tree or shrub. What else can you find?

SET UP A PITFALL TRAP

If you want to feel like the Bear Grylls of your back garden, this is a good way to start.

1 Use a trowel to dig a hole the size of a plastic cup, so that the the rim of the cup is level with the soil when you put it inside. If the cup sticks up, you won't catch anything.

2 Find pebbles, a few leaves, and some grass to put in the bottom of the cup.

3 To stop rain from filling the cup you'll need four small stones to place around its rim, and a small piece of wood to sit on top of them, making a roof over the cup.

4 Leave the trap overnight.

5 In the morning (and no later, since you don't want to harm the bugs), take off the roof and examine the contents of the cup – what creatures have wandered into it during the night?

6 Use a magnifying glass to have a closer look.

7 Return the creatures (gently) to the wild.

Older children can try painting their creatures on paper, capturing them in detail by examining their bodies with the magnifying glass.

BE AN ANT DETECTIVE

When ants find food, they leave a trail of an invisible chemical from the nest to the food source. Other worker ants then follow the trail, reinforcing it as they go. Hence the tidy lines of busy worker ants, like black-suited bureaucrats commuting through rush hour. To turn this orderly system to chaos, all you need to do is this:

1 Find an ant trail.

2 Wet your finger, then – in a gap between the ants – swipe it through the trail.

3 Watch the next ant stop short at the place you swiped.

4 Soon a whole load of ants will be circling around in confusion before they finally relocate the trail and order resumes.

Note Try following a trail back to its start (probably an underground ant complex) and to its destination (most likely a food source).

FIND A WORM'S HEAD

Not having the most expressive faces, it can sometimes be hard to tell which end is a worm's tail and which its head. If you find a worm, look for a thick band towards one end of it. It's called the saddle, and whichever end it's nearest to will be the worm's head. So now you know where to stand when talking to a worm.

FIND A BABY WOODLOUSE

I know I was fact bashing a few pages ago, but this is a really good one... woodlice are not, in fact, insects at all. They are, in reality, crustaceans! Yes, like crabs and lobsters! There's more... After mating, females carry their fertilised eggs in a small pouch under their bodies. The young then hatch inside the pouch and live in it, squirming around, until they're big enough to survive on their own, whereupon they are released and, presumably, their mother gives a massive sigh of relief.

1   Go to hunt for woodlice.

2   Since woodlice produce eggs around now, if you turn over enough of them in the spring – very gently, of course – you stand a good chance of finding a pouch of babies.

3   With a magnifying glass, look for a yellow/white sack between the front legs.

4   Turn the woodlouse back onto its front and wish it good luck.

BUILD A JAM-JAR WORMERY

They may not be the pet you've always dreamt of. They're not especially loyal, they struggle to express their love and it's hard to teach them tricks. But if you fancy keeping some worms of your very own, here's how.

1   Fill a large jar with moist soil or, even better, with alternating layers of soil and sand.

2   Put a layer of worm food on top – this could be grass cuttings, leaves and even potato peelings. Make sure all the contents are a little damp, but not waterlogged.

3   Find a few worms and plop them into the jar (no more than three, since you don't want to overcrowd them).

4   Pierce a few holes in the jam jar's lid with a skewer.

5   Put the lid on and find a dark place to keep your wormery.

6   The worms will quickly start burrowing through the layers of soil.

7   Check the wormery each day to make sure the soil is still damp, and replace any food that's going bad.

8   In a few days take out your wormery and see if you can spot any tunnels. Have the layers of soil and sand been mixed up by the movement of your worms?

9   Free your worms into the wild, where you found them.

BUILD A WOODLOUSE MAZE (AND PERFORM MAGIC)

Personal experience suggests that, if you have an indulgent grandparent, you can make a not insubstantial fortune out of this game in a single afternoon. Read on…

The science bit: if forced to make a series of turns, woodlice almost always keep turning in the opposite direction to their last turn (so that a right turn will be followed by a left turn, then a right, then a left, and so on). This instinct helps them to keep moving in a roughly 'forwards' direction, even if they have to move around lots of obstacles. So…

1   Find a collection of relatively straight twigs. They want to be thick enough that your woodlice won't automatically scale the walls.

2   A smooth surface is needed for this trick – a piece of paper on a table, or the table itself if not precious.

3   Arrange the twigs into a maze for a woodlouse. Give it lots of choices for directions in which to turn. The 'walkways' between twigs need to be large enough for a woodlouse to move through, but not wide enough for it to turn around in (so that it has to keep going forwards).

4   Sellotape the twigs so that they can't be pushed out of place.

5   Now find some woodlice. They live in damp, dark places, remember…

6   Pick up the woodlice gently with a paint brush and pop them into a jam jar before bringing them back to your maze.

7   Locate an indulgent grandparent. Tell them that you are able to communicate telepathically with your woodlice and can therefore control which way they move through the maze. Every time they turn in the direction you ask them, you must be given two pence (the going rate at the time of writing).

8   Be patient: your woodlice may scale the walls or try to sneak under twigs. If so, keep trying or find more cooperative specimens.

9   Put a woodlouse in the entrance of your maze. Watch very carefully to see which direction it turns in first, left or right.

10 If the woodlouse makes a left turn first, tell your grandparent that you have ordered it to turn right next. If it turns right, then vice versa. Then rake in the pennies as it 'obediently' moves in that direction.

11 Continue until you have worn holes in the grandparent's wallet.

Toddlers will require parental help to build the maze – something to bear in mind if you're just looking for a simple activity.

HOLD A BUG OLYMPICS

You can also use a maze to race different kinds of bug against each other. Or, organise a straight sprint by marking a starting and finishing line in the ground with a stick.

1 Collect bugs of different kinds: worms, snails, woodlice, ants...

2 Build a maze as above, but leave a wider space between the twigs to allow wider creatures like snails to pass, and create room for overtaking, too.

3 Line the bugs up at the entrance to your maze (or along your starting line), then let them all 'go' at once (some won't go at all, of course, bugs being a largely uncooperative bunch, and other, bigger specimens will immediately cheat and clamber over the walls, but as umpire you have to take a relaxed approach). The winner is whichever bug makes it to the end first, using whatever means.

Older children can, of course, think about why certain bugs are better at navigating the maze than others. What attributes are they using and how?

MAKE AN INSECT SWIMMING POOL

The day that the kids decided to build a 'swimming pool' in the garden, the result – a foil takeaway container overspilling with grubby rainwater – fell some way short of my dream. The insects, though, were less snobby. Bees stopped by, and later even some mosquitoes. Not exactly big game, sure, but we were mesmerised by our suburban safari.

1 Find a prime piece of real estate for your pool. If you want to attract bees, pick a spot near flowering plants.

2 Dig a hole the size and shape of your takeaway container, so that its edges are level with the soil.

3 Cover the bottom with soil (it'll make your pool water look scummy – more cheap motel than luxury spa – but the butterflies will enjoy the minerals in it).

4 On top of the soil, place stones of different shapes and sizes, so that some will stick up above the water for insects to land on, and others will be submerged.

5 Pour in water, making sure you don't fully cover the stones.

6 Add some stones around the edges of the pool.

7 Watch and wait to see what bugs and insects it attracts.

Older children can try their hand at wildlife photography by camping nearby with a camera, as hidden and still as possible, and try to snap the creatures at the moment they come in to drink. Or they can paint them instead.

BUILD A BUG HOTEL

I'll level with you – this isn't the Ritz. Think of it more as a motel, the kind of place a bug might rest his feelers for a night, to break up a journey across the garden. You can elaborate on the basic model, of course, to add a few more stars to its rating.

Things to bear in mind:

Amphibians like stones, bricks and old roof tiles and clay drainage tubes.

Solitary bees will be grateful for bundles of garden cane in the sunshine.

Ladybirds will enjoy piles of dry twigs and leaves later in the year when they come to hibernate.

1   Cut off the top and bottom of a plastic bottle, then cut the remaining tube into two.

2   Collect as many of the following as you can: fir cones, dry leaves, bits of bark, twigs, dead wood, straw, hay, cardboard scraps.

3   Arrange these materials by group, so that all the sticks are together, all the leaves, and so on.

4   Stuff each plastic bottle 'tube' firmly, layering up different shapes and textures until it is so tightly packed that none of the contents will slip out.

5   Leave your hotel somewhere quiet and sheltered outside.

BLOSSOM

Did you know that every year in Britain, the Queen gets a sprig of hawthorn blossom from Glastonbury as a gift? It comes from a tree whose ancestor supposedly grew from Joseph of Arimathea's own staff, more than 2,000 years ago.

Were you aware that in Japan, they've celebrated the first flowering of the cherry trees since the *5th century* with a custom called Hanami – 'flower viewing' – in which people picnic under blossom trees in their thousands? It's such a national obsession that the 'cherry blossom forecast' is released each year by the Japanese metrological office, and is tracked obsessively as it moves northwards with the warm weather, so that people planning their Hanami celebration can hit the week or two in which the blossom occurs.

And surely you've heard that the may tree, or what's also called the hawthorn, is the only British plant to be named after the month in which it blooms? It was used to decorate maypoles in the Middle Ages to celebrate the start of summer. Oh, and it's believed to be very bad luck if you bring it indoors.

No? Never mind. What is worth remembering, what really is bad luck is when you lead a straggle of suspicious kids away from their technology and towards the tow path on an unusually warm day at the very end of spring, all the way eulogising loudly about the wonders of nature above the sound of motors revving, music blaring and horns blasting.

Then you finally get them to the right spot, exhausted by your pantomime efforts at persuasion and their dragging heels, only to find a wall of nettles, beer cans and other unmentionables between you and the blossom that is the object of your 'adventure'.

You then boldly slash a path through these obstacles – watched with detached bemusement by the kids – only to find a happy band of foragers just around the corner, picking exactly the same bounty you'd been aiming for from a bush situated in the middle of an open plain, with a nice path running helpfully beside its branches.

You finally get the children to pick buckets full of the stuff and see the scepticism fade from their eyes, to be replaced by something approaching wonder. But then you realise – with dawning horror – that you have confused the blossom of the deciduous shrub Elder (really quite delicious when picked and made into cordial) with the similar-ish looking flowers of the common weed Cow Parsley (really a complete waste of an afternoon if you spend it picking and then turning it into a totally putrid cordial).

My family – making mistakes so you don't have to.

- In Japan, cherry tree blossoms symbolise the transience of life and so pop up all over the place, from art, films and music to kimonos and cutlery.
- A cow called Blossom is credited with inspiring the world's first vaccination against smallpox in the 1830s. The vaccination method proved so revolutionary that St George's Hospital, London, still keeps Blossom's hide, and even the word 'vaccination' pays homage to her, coming from the Latin *vacca*, or cow.
- Because they're light and filled with pith, Elder branches can be hollowed out to make excellent pea-shooters or, if split, boats.
- The thorns on hawthorn may be hated by kids, but they're loved by farmers since they can be grown into hedges that keep adventurous animals in their place.

TOOLKIT TO TAKE

Scissors
String
Coloured and plain paper
Double-sided sticky tape
Sellotape
Needle and thread
PVA glue
Brush
Jam jar
Paints
Tissue paper

IDEAS TO START WITH

MAKE DECORATIONS FOR AN EASTER TREE

In our house, Easter trees have a kind of lawless, anything-goes edge to them. It's hard to say if this is by dint of the short, anarchic attention spans we bring to their production each year, or whether we genuinely prefer them to look this way. It's a sort of chicken-and-Easter-egg situation.

Anyway, it goes, roughly and messily, like this:

1   Go out, and hunt down some fallen sticks and twigs.

2   Put the sticks and twigs in a vase at home to make the basis of your tree and hang decorations from.

3   Sprigs found intact can be added to the vase whole, sticks can be painted in bright colours.

4   Next, hunt for blossom.

5   Remove petals from any blossom that's been bashed about.

6   Glue the petals to paper shapes (stars, or whatever shapes you fancy).

7   Some of the shapes can then be painted, beautifully or otherwise.

8   Thread a needle and pierce each shape near the top, drawing the thread through.

9   Tie each thread into a loop, so the decorations can be hung.

10 Hang the decorations on your twig tree.

11 Have a piece of cake.

Toddlers When little ones are involved the paper can be precut into easy, non-fiddly shapes, and the blossom applied with an abstract abandon (think Jackson Pollock in petals).

Older children can get more ambitious. They could cut the paper into the shape of a chick, for instance, and try recreating the texture of feathers with the petals, or cut the paper into a basic rectangle and use petals of different shades to create the contours and colours of the image itself.

CREATE A BLOSSOM SNOWSTORM

Need to blow off some steam? The following activity is not rocket science, but it is a tried and tested method of preventing the expulsion of excess energy on siblings and soft furnishings instead.

1   Hunt for blossom on the ground. AS MUCH AS YOU CAN! A TON PREFERABLY! RUN, RUN, RUN!

2   Separate the petals (we REALLY don't want any sprigs, twigs or branches, thanks).

3   Gather fistfuls of petals.

4   Hurl the petals into the air as high as you can and (again) RUN, RUN, RUN in circles and mad shapes, tossing them about and trying to keep as many as possible in the air as you go.

5   Collapse on the floor. Job done.

MAKE A BLOSSOM CROWN

If you have, or are, an older child, this can indeed be made into a delicate, beautiful halo. If you have, or are, a toddler, well… forget about that aspect, but this can (with a little bit of creative licence and imagination) be variously reinvented to suit most purposes and obsessions. To date, in our house we've made fairy crowns, camouflage headgear, and the Supper King Crown (awarded to the best or paciest consumer of vegetables).

1 Cut the shape of a crown from paper. This can be a basic hoop, or have a row of points and detail at the front – whatever your imagination and scissor skills dictate, but remember to loop the paper around the wearer's head first, to make sure you cut it to size. You may need to use tape to stick together two pieces of paper.

2 Hunt for blossom. If you find different shapes, sizes and colours, then great – you can use them for details (cream blossom for the gold parts, pink petals for jewels, perhaps?).

3 Glue the blossom to your crown. If you're working with a diminutive person or attention span, strips of double-sided sticky tape take less time and precision.

4 When you've added as much detail and covered as much of the paper as you fancy, use double-sided sticky tape to loop and stick the paper into a hoop.

5 Voila! Your finished crown (or camouflage, or bandana, or….).

Note If you have thick wire to hand, you can bend it into a head-sized loop before threading whole heads of blossom onto it for a 'Frida Kahlo' effect. Just twist the ends together at the end.

MAKE A SPRING GARLAND

We sometimes cheat at this and just use cut flowers hanging around the house if they're starting to look a bit dead and we're feeling a bit comatose, too. But blossom is best. Much brighter and more beautiful.

1 Hunt for blossom on the ground. It's nice – but absolutely not essential – to have a selection of some whole flowers and some loose petals.

2 Spread them out and decide on the order that you'd like to thread them onto your garland. Do you want blocks of colour or a random rainbow? Sprigs at regular intervals between petals or a chaos of shapes?

3 Thread a needle, and measure out the length of thread according to how long you want your garland to be. Fold a square of Sellotape over the end, so things don't fall off it.

4 Pierce the thickest part of the first flower or petal, and gently pull the thread through.

5 Keep going, piercing the thickest parts of the flowers if you can, and thinking about the amount of space you want to leave between them until you've threaded your last flower (or your fingers ache).

6 Fold another square of Sellotape over the other end of the thread.

7 Hang the garland. It'll be just as nice when the petals dry.

Toddlers will have to be careful, clearly, with fingers and fiddly needles and thread. Still, under the right conditions, this is actually a pretty good way of practising the skill, as well as concentration and coordination more generally.

MAKE A BLOSSOM MOBILE

Follow the same steps as for the garland, only…

1   You'll need to string petals onto four shorter lengths of thread instead of one longer one. Tie a little knot after each petal if you're worried about them slipping.

2   Now make the frame to hang the petals from. Find two straight-ish sticks.

3   Arrange the sticks into a cross (one on top of the other, pointing in opposite directions).

4   Wrap string tightly around the place where the sticks cross until it's secure. Then knot it, leaving a length of spare string. Now you have the frame.

5   Create a loop with the spare length of string and tie it. This is what your mobile will hang from.

6   Tie a thread of petals from each of the four ends of the cross.

7   You're done!

BLOSSOM PRESSING

Look, there are fancier, more fail-safe ways of doing this, but if you're just up for tinkering about, and don't have all the snazzy kit, then this is the method for you. It'll work perfectly fine and look very sweet, and won't involve queuing in a craft shop while your toddler tips turpentine off the display shelves. Oh, and it's free.

1   Hunt for blossom.

2   Make sure the blossom is *dry*, otherwise you'll get mould. Less pretty.

3   Find a big, heavy book. Open it and place some tissue paper flat on a page.

4   Place the petals on the tissue paper. Try to avoid the edges of the book to get an even press.

5   Place another sheet of tissue paper over the top, then close the book.

6   Put something heavy on top of the book, and leave for *four weeks*.

7   Open up and admire your flowers. Then do any one of a million interesting things with them (use them as confetti; glue them to jam jars, then stick a tea light inside to make a lantern; stick them to paper and make bookmarks or wrapping paper; turn them into collages).

Older children If they want to be doubly careful and professional, they can try changing the tissue paper and book every week. It can help remove the moisture from the petals.

CREATE A BLOSSOM COLLAGE

1 Hunt for blossom – different shades and shapes if you can find them.

2 Take out a piece of paper, glue and a brush.

3 Stir your imagination: what can you depict using only blossom (no crayons or paint allowed)? A lion's furry mane and face? A tree? You can find sticks, too, to make its trunk and branches. The pink clouds of a sunset sky?

4 Get gluing.

Note You can always make your collage on a flat bit of ground outside and ditch the paper – no gluing required.

MAKE ELDERFLOWER CORDIAL

This one's an added extra, a bonus track if you will. It's a sneaky, unofficial activity because it calls for a few very simple things that aren't on the official toolkit list (a saucepan, for one, and lemons and sugar). But we couldn't let this section end without it, because spring always ends, for us, with cordial.

1 Pick the elderflowers – you're aiming for 25 heads of the stuff.

2 Rinse the flowers of any small imposters (bugs).

3 Put 1 kg (2¼ lb) sugar and 1.5 litres (1¾ pints) of water in a pan, heat gently until the sugar has dissolved, then bring to the boil before turning off the heat.

4 Add the flowers to the pan along with the grated zest of three lemons and their juice.

5 Stir, then cover with a big plate and leave for 24 hours.

6 Stir, then strain through a muslin cloth (or just use a piece of kitchen towel inside a sieve) into a bottle or jug.

Note You can add citric acid to make the cordial last. We never have it around the house so we just leave it out and drink the cordial faster. No great hardship.

MAKE BLOSSOM PERFUME

Bubble, bubble, toil and trouble… If you are five there is no better cause to which to devote an afternoon than using a stick to mash petals (and anything else you can get your hands on) into a gratifyingly gross pulp. If you're an infinitely more sophisticated 11, playing properly at being a perfumier involves a mature approach but, essentially, the same methods.

1 Hunt for blossom – different kinds, ideally.

2 Hold up the blossom flowers to your nose to analyse their scents, first individually, then in combinations – which do you prefer? Which complement others best?

3 When you've settled on the combination for your signature scent, put the petals in a jam jar, add water and pound with a stick.

4 Keep smelling as you go. Does it need a whisper more cherry blossom? A note of hawthorn? Add accordingly.

5 The more you pound, the more intense the smell will be. Equally, if you're patient enough to leave the mixture overnight, you'll find its scent has deepened.

6 Dab it on for a subtle scent, or drench yourself in it if you're more the dramatic than discreet sort.

TRY THE BLOSSOM 'YOGA' MOVE

1 Lie flat on your back, with your arms stretched up above your head. Breathe in slowly and deeply.

2 Breathing out, sit up slowly, with your arms remaining stretched up till they are pointing at the sky.

3 Bend forwards to your toes and rest for a moment.

4 Slowly and carefully sit up, then lie back down on the floor, your arms still stretched up above your head.

5 Repeat until you reach a karmic state of total peace (or your stomach starts to rumble).

Note If it starts to feel like hard work or there's even a whisper of it hurting anywhere in your body, stop immediately.

SUMMER

Our summers are truly something out of a George Gershwin song. Sure, the fish come battered, not jumping, around us. And while the neighbours are occasionally high, the cotton never is. But the outdoor living is easy. As the summer months slide by, we slip naturally into the habit of hanging out all day under the sky until, finally, it looks ablaze with a million chimney fires, the city's rooftops backlit in fuchsia and gold.

In the summer I can almost kid myself that I've got this outdoors business covered. I can *almost* get a bit smug. So the children aren't exactly walking on England's mountains green, nor, come to think of it, have they its pleasant pastures seen. Not much, not recently... but we're out there dashing and squealing and spreading out under the sky.

Except, except, except... When I consciously tried to concoct some good, clean fun, my ideas rarely seemed to match the kids'. The problem may have been in the definition. I'd see cute, camera-ready 'craft activities' on Pinterest and – with the best of intentions but the littlest of sense – would attempt to recreate them. Unfortunately I didn't have biddable babies to work with. I had a wild, wilful gang that was waging war on the very principles of 'good' and 'clean'.

Forget the fact that the thing I had in mind was supposed to make mini Matisses of them all. The minute I had emptied out all the cupboards and retrieved the obscure paraphernalia required (a pipette, air-drying clay *and* a laminator?!) they discovered something

infinitely more absorbing under a nearby log – a fossilising poo, for example, to be prodded with a stick till teatime.

That work, they could concentrate on for hours, with an intensity and industry I'd never managed to apply to any real, adult job I'd done myself. But ask them to take part in the project I'd painstakingly pieced together? Thirty seconds, max.

I still wanted them to look beyond the primary-coloured playground tiles to the real wilderness on their fringes, but something had to go. It was either my sanity or the parental hovering over prescriptive activities. And in the end I decided that dispensing with the latter was the course of action I'd least likely come to regret.

So we tried something new and put away the pipettes and the laminators, alongside my best-laid plans. Instead, we threw our least dangerous bits of kitchen equipment into a bag with some scruffy art supplies from the toy box, went outside and found some flowers. They opened the bag. I opened a magazine. I read and the kids did... God knows what. It didn't matter. Whatever it was, they did it for 40 whole minutes, with total dedication and without interrupting my reading. Happy kids, happy mother. We did it again, and again. Sometimes they would happily mastermind their own shady schemes; at others their imaginations would require a small kick-start. On some occasions I would get lost with them inside the worlds they wove. On others, materials given and idea planted, I would sit back and read at at least a chapter before looking up. And that, dear reader, was the beginning of a beautiful thing.

FACT BOX

- Three- to five-year-olds have lost an average of eight and a half hours of unstructured play each week, according to a University of Michigan study tracking time usage from 1981 to 1997. Their older siblings, aged six to eight years, lost an average of nearly four hours.
- Nearly half of the children questioned in a survey by Natural England stated that they were not allowed to play outside unsupervised, and nearly a quarter were worried about being out alone.
- Psychologists from the German University of Hildesheim found that people given lots of free, unstructured playtime as children have more supportive and fulfilling social lives as adults.
- Dr Stuart Brown's analysis of 6,000 'play histories' suggests that children deprived of unstructured play often become adults who are 'rigid, humourless, inflexible and closed to trying out new options' (we all know one of them), while child-led free play 'enhances the capacity to innovate, adapt and master changing circumstances'.
- Children's need for free play time is considered so fundamental that it is written into the UN Convention of the Rights of the Child. Article 31 states that 'every child has the right to rest and leisure'.
- A report by the All Party Parliamentary Group on a Fit and Healthy Childhood in 2015 confirmed the importance of unstructured play: 'children learn and develop both while playing and through play – they are both learning how to cope with the immediate world around them and, at the same time, acquiring skills that will serve them well in the future'.

BUTTERFLIES AND MOTHS

It's mid-July and I am crouched low behind some plant pots in the garden, accompanied by several mildly catatonic children, when our neighbour's head floats up over the fence. 'What are you doing?' asks the head. 'Hiding from, and watching for, butterflies,' I reply. 'Why?' 'Because David Attenborough told us to.' 'How long have you been sitting like that?' A child pipes up: '*Days.* We've run out of snacks and we are *probably* starving to death.' 'Why don't you have a little break?' suggests the slightly confused head, 'they're not going anywhere.'

And so we have a break (accompanied, in the traditional manner, by a Kit-Kat), while doing an odd dance to shake the cramp from our legs. The kids go back to terrorising the flower beds while I start thinking... *well, are they? Going anywhere, I mean?* And, thus – though the hunt itself is aborted and, in the words of one child, is 'a big fat fail'– we nonetheless glean the following:

1   They are! Going somewhere, that is. According to the most recent count, over 40 per cent of Britain's resident butterfly species are under threat, making them one of our most rapidly declining wildlife groups.

2   This is bad for the butterflies, clearly, but also for the rest of us. Says Sir David: 'Butterflies are a key indicator species of the health of our environment – if they are struggling, then many other species are struggling also.' He's right. According to the State of Nature report, published in 2013 by the UK's leading wildlife groups, 60 per cent of our native species are in decline, while one in ten are heading for total disappearance from our fair isle.

3   While you should never question anything that Sir David, in his infinite wisdom, decrees (he has his reasons) there are more fun ways to interact with butterflies than crouching behind a row of plastic pots until your children are looking daggers at you and your feet are shooting them up your legs.

To that end, we joined a group of children volunteering at Vauxhall City Farm, a muddy oasis squatting incongruously beneath the monumental shadow of the MI6 building, headquarters of the British Secret Intelligence Service.

Now, city farms are wonderful things: community-run smallholdings, often surrounded by high-rise buildings and concrete, with a mission to introduce and involve urban communities in food production and farming. There are 60 across the UK and in one I once saw a group of primary school children shrink in fear at the sight of a goose before a plump and plucky little girl stepped forwards, pointed at its long neck and shrieked, 'Oh my God. It's a giraffe!'

At Vauxhall, though, the kids are happily getting stuck in, shovelling pony poo. They learn by doing, explains their supervisor Laura McMahon, they take pride in even their smellier tasks, and they don't just celebrate the cute and cuddly creatures, either.

Across the yard from the fluffy alpacas and the pretty ponies is the 'ecology garden' – a temple to bugs, beetles and butterflies. The children built its bug hotel, constructed its 'rain temple' and planted the wild meadow on its roof, a haven for butterflies in a world where its wild habitats are rapidly disappearing.

'Kids come back every year,' says Laura. How sad if one day, they were met with a meadow empty of butterflies.

FACTS TO FIRE THE IMAGINATION

- There are somewhere between 12,000 and 20,000 species of butterfly in the world.
- Moths are even more numerous: about 160,000 species have been counted worldwide.
- Every year, some Monarch butterflies in the US travel more than 4,000 km (2,485 miles) to lay their eggs before a new generation travels all the way back, completing the cycle.
- The fastest butterflies in the world – skippers – can fly 60 km (37 miles) per hour. Most butterflies stick to between 8 and19 km (5–12 miles) an hour.
- Some butterflies and moths are poisonous. The Cinnabar Moth caterpillar feeds on poisonous ragwort leaves and as a result is inedible to birds, both as a caterpillar and as a butterfly.
- An average adult butterfly has a life span of around a month.

TOOLKIT TO TAKE

Paper plate
String
Scissors
Takeaway container
Paper
Crayons
White cloth
Paint brush
A large jam jar (the size that
    mayonnaise or gherkins come in)

IDEAS TO START WITH

BUILD A BUTTERFLY FEEDER

Patience is not a virtue that overflows in our family gene pool. So when butterfly spotting, we like to tip the odds gently in our favour. It's not cheating. Not exactly. We prefer to call it ingenuity.

1   Take a paper plate and pierce four equally spaced holes in its rim (as if you were picking out the corners of a square).

2   Cut four equal lengths of string and thread them through the holes.

3   Then tie a knot in the bottom of each piece of string, underneath the plate, so that the string doesn't slip out.

4   Gather the other ends of the strings and tie them together in a knot.

5   Hang this feeder from a branch, near some flowers.

6   It is now ready to be loaded up with butterfly food. Got any over-ripe fruits you were thinking of chucking out? Those will do nicely.

7   Watch for visitors!

MISLEAD A BUTTERFLY

A bit mean, this one, since you're effectively luring male butterflies with the false hope of romance. It feels a little like creating a hideously misleading online-dating profile.

1 Take a piece of white cloth and tear it into small, oblong scraps (about the same height as a butterfly but twice as long).

2 Now find a spot with lots of flowers to attract butterflies and a bit of a breeze blowing through it.

3 Tie the cloth scraps all around the area – to branches and stalks, around flowers and leaves... wherever you can.

4 Now hide. As the scraps flutter in the breeze, the poor male butterflies belonging to species that are white in colour will mistake them for potential love interests and fly over. You'll get a great view (and a heavy conscience). Don't forget to take them down afterwards to give the poor guys a break.

MAKE A BUTTERFLY PUDDLE

1 Fill a takeaway container with soil. It's rich in the minerals butterflies need.

2 Add water to turn the soil into a muddy slop.

3 Place some stones in your puddle, to give the butterflies places to rest, and add a couple of slices of old fruit to tempt them further.

4 Place your 'butterfly puddle' somewhere surrounded by flowers.

5 Wait to see if visitors land for a drink.

6 Remember to top up the puddle with water daily.

Older children will also enjoy learning why butterflies *can* drink from muddy puddles but *can't* drink water from ponds: because the surface tension on water is too strong for their delicate wings.

WATCH A BUTTERFLY RUN ITS ERRANDS

What does a butterfly's diary look like? Where does the Silver Spotted Skipper do its supermarket shop? How does a Large White loosen up? Does nature have a nursery where the Northern Brown Angus can drop her newborns? These are the pressing questions we set out to answer.

1 Sit still and quietly somewhere where there are lots of flowers to tempt a butterfly. Don't panic if you don't have a garden – a window box will do nicely.

2 When you spot a butterfly, watch its movements carefully, looking for the following:

- **Which plants attract the most butterflies?**

- **Can you see a butterfly sunbathing?** Butterflies fly at their best when they reach a temperature of around 28 °C (82 °F). When it's significantly cooler, you'll see them opening their wings to warm themselves in the sun.

- **Do you see any 'puddling' going on?** Look for groups of butterflies congregating on the edges of muddy or sandy patches. They're drinking up the salts and minerals and they'll mostly be males. It's kind of like a Friday night at the pub.

- **Can you see any 'nectaring'?** That's eating, basically, except that butterflies don't have chewing mouth parts. Instead they sip nectar through a straw on the head called the 'proboscis', which they can insert deep into a flower.

- **How about some mating?** Birds do it, bees do it, even educated fleas do it… And butterflies, too, so keep a lookout.

- **What about egg laying?** If you spot a butterfly landing on a leaf for a few seconds before flying off, go and inspect the leaf. It may have laid eggs. If so, they'll be tiny and off-white or yellow coloured.

INCUBATE A CATERPILLAR

If you've got a child who's more into 'urrgghhhh!' than 'ahhhhh!' – more excited by creepy-crawly caterpillars, basically, than beautiful butterflies – then welcome to the club and this might be the activity for you.

Note You need a jar that's larger than a jam jar – a large mayonnaise or gherkin jar will do nicely.
Another note We are talking about living creatures here, so you really need to commit to looking after your caterpillars for the whole of this process if you're going to give this a shot.

1   First make some holes in the lid of the jar (if you can't make holes, make sure you take the lid off every day during the caterpillar stage, so that the caterpillars get enough air). A piece of fabric held on with a rubber band is a good alternative lid.

2   Make a floor of damp soil on the bottom, and add a couple of sticks that the caterpillar can climb up.

2   Now you need to find your caterpillars. It's worth checking which caterpillars are most common in your area because you can then check the flowers that they love best ('host plants').

3   Don't forget to check the undersides of leaves and look at ones that are curled up. Damaged leaves are also a sign that a caterpillar may have been munching nearby.

4   When you find a few caterpillars, lift them gently with a paint brush, then lower them into the jar along with leaves from the plant you found them on.

5   Make a note of this plant – caterpillars are picky and yours will want to eat this particular one from now on.

6   Put the lid on the jar and take it inside. Keep it somewhere out of direct sunlight.

7   Check moisture levels in the jar every day and replenish the leaves.

8   Watch and wait as the caterpillars get bigger and fatter, even shedding their skins until, if you're lucky...

9   They turn into chrysalises! They might hang off the underside of the lid now but don't worry, you don't need to remove it to feed them at this stage.

10 Just keep a very close eye until the chrysalises hatch into butterflies.

11 Take the jar outside as soon as this happens, remove the lid and watch the butterflies fly into the wild.

Older children, with a bit of guidance, can try to identify host plants. Here are some of the best: fuchsias, holly, honeysuckle, ivy, Primrose, Sweet Rocket and verbascum.

HAVE A COLOUR COMPETITION

This is not a 'rocket-science' activity. This is an 'Oh, Lord, I've got too many kids with too much energy, but also too little time to drum up anything sophisticated' sort of activity. Not that it's any the worse for that.

1   Throw the children outside, somewhere where there are lots of flowers.

2   Tell them that the child who spots the most butterflies of different colours – red, white, green and so on – gets an ice cream, or the title of Butterfly King, or universal respect and adoration, whatever works for you.

3   Watch them dash about in a frenzy.

DRAW A BUTTERFLY BEFORE IT FLIES AWAY

This activity can either be a furious race against the clock, a competition between friends or a peaceful artistic pursuit, depending on the people you bring to it.

1 Camp out near a flower bed with crayons and paper at the ready.

2 When a butterfly lands, try to draw it as best you can before it flies off.

3 The winner is the person who best captures its shape, colours and patterns in the time available.

TRY THE BUTTERFLY 'YOGA' POSE

1 Sit somewhere peaceful with a straight back and your feet stretched out in front of you.

2 Bend your knees and bring your feet in towards you, so that the soles lie flat against each other.

3 Take a deep, slow breath, counting to ten.

4 As you breathe out, try to gently lower your knees slightly towards the ground.

5 As you inhale, bring your knees up slowly again.

6 Repeat this process, slowly moving your knees up and down, as if they were flapping like the wings of a butterfly.

FLOWERS

There are children who are possessed of an innate appreciation of the beauty of flowers – who value them for their delicate scent, blushing petals and velvety leaves. I know, I've met them.

There are others, though, whose interaction with flowers is more… physical. For whom a carefully tended flower bed is a terrain through which to charge an imaginary army or on which to land a football. These are the ones who gravitate to my house. Over time I've come to attach names to these camps. There's the former, henceforth known as the 'flower *child*', and the latter, hereafter labelled the 'flower *power*'.

Apparently, though – the safety and symmetry of your decorative dahlia beds aside – it really doesn't matter which type your child typically is, or which persona she happens to be adopting today. The point is simply the flowers.

In 2011 the University of Tennessee began studying a typical playground, with the usual wooden and plastic play equipment. The research was conducted by one Dawn Coe, a woman with the mixed blessing of a job title so lengthy that it is punctuated with two pauses for breath: 'Assistant Professor in the Department of Kinesiology, Recreation and Sport Studies'.

For months, Coe dutifully noted down the frequency, duration and intensity with which the children used the slides, monkey bars and so on. Then the playground got a makeover. They planted little trees, added a creek, rocks, logs and flowers. Meanwhile, Coe and her notebook stayed on.

It turned out that the flowers and the rest of the 'natural playscape' had a big effect. The children stayed outside, playing, for more than twice as long as they had before. Their games, from jumping off logs to watering the flowers, were also more aerobic and strengthening.

Okay, so this doesn't give you scientifically sound, proven, unshakeable and universally applicable findings about play (and isn't the *point* of play that it defies these?). The findings, however, strongly suggest the following. Having flowers (and other forms of nature) where children play makes it:

1   More fun than it is when you just have a pile of toys and equipment designed for the purpose by an adult whose memories of imaginative play are so distant that it takes a double espresso and a glance at the credit-card statement to kickstart them into action.

2   Healthier than playing with just the aforementioned equipment.

3   Longer lasting than it would be if you were only playing with that equipment, thereby giving parents more time to get on with 'important' stuff (double macchiato drinking and bank-balance checking).

Oh, and in the US, play equipment comes in at around $1,000 per child, that's about £655. Seed packets, on the other hand, cost around 33p (or 50 cents) in my local garden centre. This makes flowers quite a bit less burdensome on that bank balance, too, so adults might have to work less hard to pay for them and possibly, in theory, could have a little more time to play among the petals themselves.

FACTS TO FIRE THE IMAGINATION

- Flowers first appeared on the Earth 140 million years ago.
- In the 1600s tulips were more valuable than gold in Holland.
- Orchids do not need soil to grow – some get nutrients from soil fungi, some from moisture and some from the air.
- Sunflowers produce toxic substances that suppress other plants around them. This property is called allelopathy.
- Carnivorous plants eat insects and other small animals! When one lands on the little hairs on their leaves, the trap snaps shut and digestive juices break it down. You've probably heard of some of the more exotic carnivorous plants found around the world, like Venus Fly Traps. But there are UK plants that also lure, trap, and digest insects, like sundews and butterworts.
- In 2015, a flower said to be the world's largest bloomed in Tokyo, Japan. The Titan arum was 2 m (6½ ft) high and is known as 'the corpse flower' because of its nasty smell.

TOOLKIT TO TAKE

Scissors
Paper
PVA glue
Brush
Paints
Jam jar
Tissue paper
Sellotape
String
Paper plate
Double-sided sticky tape
Magnifying glass
Needle and thread
Candles
Blu-tack

IDEAS TO START WITH

DISSECT A FLOWER

In our experience, one of very few activities through which the two types – 'flower *child*' and 'flower *power*' – can find happy common ground.

1 Find a flower – ideally a big one, so that the parts are easily visible.

2 Take a white or pale piece of paper and stick a length of the double-sided tape all the way down the middle of it. Peel off the back so you can stick and display flower parts as you go.

3 Remove the petals and stick them to the paper.

4 Once all the petals are off, you'll get a good view of the pistil (the female parts) and stamen (male parts that contain the pollen).

5 Add the stamen to your paper. Don't worry if lots of the pollen comes off.

6 Then add the pistil.

7 Take a good look at everything through a magnifying glass.

Toddlers With little ones scale back on the science and don't worry about the naming of the parts. Unless they ask, of course.

Older children can use the dissection to think about the science of pollination.

MAKE A RAINBOW FLOWER

I know, I know: you can't improve on nature. But try telling that to a six-year-old who has created the mother of all multicoloured monstrosities.

1 Go flower hunting. You want to use as many different-coloured flowers as possible, remembering to leave some for nature.

2 Remove the petals from the flowers.

3 Paste PVA glue over a big-ish portion of a piece of paper.

4 On the wet glue, arrange the petals from your various flowers into one big, multicoloured super-flower.

5 Leave to dry.

6 Give to Granny.

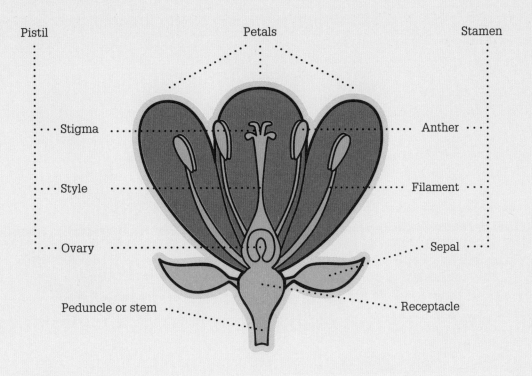

Pistil · Petals · Stamen

· · · Stigma · Anther · · ·

· · · Style · Filament · · ·

· · · Ovary · Sepal · · ·

Peduncle or stem · Receptacle

TRY FLOWER PRINTING

This is a bit like potato printing, only a bit less precise. And messier. If you hate mess, and are accompanied by a child whose enthusiasm outweighs their carefulness by a ratio of more than 3 to 1, this might not be for you. Just a warning.

1 Find flowers. You're going to cover them in paint, then press them against paper to leave their shapes imprinted, so flat-faced flowers* (like daisies and dandelions) will be easier to work with than conical ones like tulips. But really, it's up to you.

2 When you've got your collection of flowers, use a brush to coat one in paint, then carefully press the painted side against a piece of paper.

3 Peel off the flower carefully from the paper and see whether you've managed to leave its shape behind.

4 Now try your other flowers, in other colours of paint.

*Not the technical term, I am aware, but if you came here looking for those you most probably gave up at page 2, anyway...

Older children with longer attention spans could try folding their sheets of paper into quarters in order to cut out a series of smaller rectangles. Print onto these and leave them to dry before sellotaping them to a length of string to make bunting. You can make good greetings cards from these too.

COLOUR TREASURE HUNT

Would you like, just once, to read the Sunday paper? Maybe not the whole paper, but at least a colour supplement. Well, now you can! It takes a tiny bit of prep the night before, but honestly, it's very straightforward (nothing that can't be done after a couple of glasses of wine). The following day, take the kids to the park, set them this treasure hunt to do, then sit on a blanket, spread out the papers and... go!

1 In advance of the game, someone who will not be playing it (that's you, Dad) needs to cut a piece of paper into strips, then paint or colour each a different colour – a brief squiggle will do.

2 When you're ready to play, each child should be given a pile of cards, including the full range of colours (it's also fine if there's only one child, anything goes).

3 The challenge is to find a natural thing that matches the colour on each card (most likely a flower for the brighter colours, but if your palate is a bit murky then bark, twigs and the like can be included).

4 Shout 'Go!' and watch the children scatter. Now read your newspaper. Quickly.

MAKE A SUMMER STAINED GLASS WINDOW

The world's most famous stained glass is probably that of Sainte Chapelle, in the centre of Paris, which has roughly 600 m² (6,458 ft²) of intricately patterned coloured glass in its upper chapel. This is a lot but, I'd argue, not a great deal more than we have in our house during the summer, plastered across every window or glass surface, secured with little squares of masking tape that remain, dotted around the place, for months after the artworks' removal. Here's how we do it.

1   Go out hunting for leaves and petals. These will make the multicoloured patterns of your stained glass, so select the most colourful hues you can find.

2   Take out the palest colour of tissue paper at your disposal. Very strong or dark colours simply aren't going to work, I'm afraid.

3   Decide what pattern you are going to create with your leaves and petals. They are going to lie flat against the tissue paper, so discard anything that sticks out very far *at all*, and use individual petals rather than whole flowers.

4   Using a brush and a very delicate touch, sweep the petals with glue and press them lightly onto the tissue paper (toddlers might need help here, as both tissue paper and petals have a horrible habit of crumpling up and tearing).

5   Once you've finished gluing your pattern leave it to dry, then...

6   Hold up the tissue paper to a window. You can experiment to see which way round you prefer it: petals facing out, or petals sandwiched between the tissue paper and the glass.

7   When you've found a spot in which the paper catches the light and are happy with how it looks, use your Sellotape (or masking tape) to attach it to the window. Voila! Your own Sainte Chapelle.

Older children seeking more inspiration can have a look at other famous pieces of stained glass around the world, for example in the Chicago Cultural Center, the Swiss Grossmünster Church, the Netherlands Institute for Sounds and Vision, York Minster, and Matisse's Chapelle du Rosaire in France.

MAKE A JAM-JAR LANTERN

1   Go out hunting for nice, flatten-able petals.

2   Paint the outside of a jam jar with PVA glue.

3   Now stick your petals onto the jar.

4   Leave to dry.

5   Once dry, paint another layer of PVA glue over the jam jar, petals and all.

6   When fully dried, you can stick a tea-light or stubby candle inside the jar – once lit, the flame will glow through your petals.

MAKE A MANDALA

So you're dreaming of spending your summer holiday on some exotic south Indian beach. Meanwhile, you're stuck on your staycation Saffron Walden. Again. You have my sympathies. Why not create your very own piece of exotic Buddhist art? Maybe it will transport you imaginatively to your own far-eastern paradise island. Maybe....

1   Collect flat leaves and petals in as many shades as you can.

2   Fetch a paper plate on which to glue them.

3   Decide what cosmic diagram you want to create with them. Traditionally, mandalas take the form of geometric designs intended to symbolise the universe.

4   Using a brush, very lightly sweep your first petal with glue and press it delicately onto the plate. Continue until you've attached all the elements of your design.

5   When the mandala is fixed and dry, jab a hole in the top of the plate.

6   Thread a piece of string through the hole and tie it into a loop. You can now hang up your mandala.

7   Try to feel zen.

Older children can make a mandala that catches the light by cutting out the centre of the plate and replacing it with tissue paper. Then glue their design onto this. Once it's dry, they can hang it near a window so the light streams through the petals and their background.

MAKE A FLOWER FIGURE

So far I've asked you to remove a lot of petals from flowers. 'But what about the bits that are left?!' I hear you clamour. Well. Here's what. When we started robbing flowers of their petals, we realised that quite a lot of them looked like little bald heads on a body – only without arms, which seemed a bit sad, so we gave them transplants made from twigs and it just spiralled from there.

1 Take a bald flowerhead on a stem.

2 Find a very thin, straight twig to be your flower's arms. Snap it to the length you think the arms should be.

3 Use a length of thread to tie the twig to the flower's stem, two-thirds of the way up.

4 Now dress your figure. A leaf can make a good dress: fold it in half, then cut a hole in the centre of the fold, big enough to slip over the flower's head and rest over its twiggy arms. Then tie it at the 'waist' with some thread. You can also use Blu-tack to attach the clothes. To top off their outfit add a grass wig or leaf hat.

TRY THE FLOWER 'YOGA' POSE

....

1 Sit on the floor with a straight back, as if you were crossing your knees but with the soles of your feet touching instead.

2 Breathe in and put your hands under your ankles.

3 Breathe out, and lift your feet and shins off the floor, keeping your back straight and your knees sticking out.

4 Breathe in, and lower them to the ground again.

SAND AND SHELLS

It's a chilly British evening and I'm sitting at my desk in my slippers, staring at the Californian beach that's flashed up on my computer screen. In the foreground is a sandy cliff-side track; behind it there's a sky unfeasibly wide and blue, and a sun beating down on an implausibly turquoise sea. I take a sip of tea and try not to hate the man taunting me with this image: Gever Tulley, the American founder of Tinkering School, with whom I am having a Skype conversation from my gloomy attic.

'I don't think we have to go back to living in the woods,' he explains, 'but I do think that as a culture we need to decide what the equivalent cultural experience is to that autonomy children had a couple of decades ago, even if we live in the city. It's one of my mission statements.'

Tinkering School, his answer to that challenge, holds week-long summer camps on 'a big ranch, in a little canyon' just a couple of miles from the sea. Here, children aged from eight to 18 are set a project on arrival. 'For instance,' says Gever, his eyes glittering, 'here's an abandoned sandy railway, on a cliff overlooking the sea. We have wind. We have a track. What can we build with those resources, to carry us all the way down that track, so that we can have pizza at the place at the end?'

The answer that the kids cooked up flashes, now, onto my screen: a photo of a sail-powered rail car. Over a week, it was designed by the kids, sawed by the kids, hammered by the kids, tested by the kids, found at fault by the kids, tinkered with by the kids and, finally, ridden all the way down the track by the kids, the sand kicking up into their faces, the wind tunnelling through their T-shirts and the salty air slapping their cheeks as they raced past the Pacific Ocean.

Other groups have built rollercoasters and gliders. They have used power tools. They have flown, sped and tumbled from their own creations. Which just leaves me with one question... how?! How have these kids designed, built and... well, *concentrated* for long enough to create these masterpieces of engineering? And how have they emerged with all their fingers and toes intact?

Gever shrugs. Before each camp, he and his staff come up with the goal the kids will be set that week. Then, they decide what materials to bring to the ranch. 'Between these tools and these materials,' says Gever, 'we know the kids will be able to make something that fits with the aim.'

The idea is to 'do just the right amount of planning to make it happen, then let the students take the reins. My ideas are never perfect, I always trust the kids to shape their evolution.'

Bring the right idea, the right materials and the right degree of trust, and the rest, he says, comes free. And by the rest, he means 'engaged, discovery-based, self-motivated, self-challenging learning'.

Besides, these experiences at camp may look risky, but the alternative might be more dangerous. Gever says they are the building blocks of competence and safety, skills that, in his opinion, 'schools don't really teach', while exams 'just measure what we can memorise'. A bubble-wrapped child, he says, can't be expected to grow up to change the world, 'and we owe it to our kids to help them see the world's complexities and dangers as something wonderful and worth making better.'

'One of the kids who built the sail-powered rail car asked me what I hoped she would get from it. I said I hoped she would become the kind of person you would choose to be shipwrecked with – a competent person, one who'd never give up, and could build her own escape method and who'd never stop trying to survive. You know, I think we should all try to be that sort of person: competent, resourceful and resilient; cheerful and playful; tenacious and curious.'

FACTS TO FIRE THE IMAGINATION

- The wind can make whole sand dunes migrate. Carrying the finer grains and bouncing bigger ones along, gusts can move dunes up to a record-breaking 100 m (328 ft) a year.
- Sand dunes exist on other planets, too. There are sand dunes on Mars, Venus and Titan, Saturn's moon.
- One estimate puts the number of grains of sand on the world's beaches at seven quintillion, five hundred quadrillion grains. Since there are an estimated 70 thousand million, million, million stars in the universe, there are probably more grains of sand on our beaches than stars in the sky.
- All sand originates from just three sources – rocks, organisms and minerals – but every single grain is unique. Though sand looks yellow, under a microscope the grains are an infinite variety of shapes and colours.
- Shells are the skeletons of a class of marine animals called molluscs. We mammals have our skeletons on the insides of our bodies, but molluscs have their skeletons on the outside.

TOOLKIT TO TAKE

String
PVA glue
Brushes
Coloured paper
Crayons
Scissors
Trowel
Jam jar
Paper
Blu-tack
Bucket and spade, if you have them to hand

IDEAS TO START WITH

BUILD A SANDCASTLE

Do you want the scientifically proven formula for building the perfect sandcastle? OW=0.125xS. Any the wiser? Scientists at Bournemouth University claim that, where S represents the weight of sand in grams and OW the optimum level of water required, you need eight parts sand to one part water to make a peerless castle.

1. Find some damp – but not wet – sand (the magic ratio is 8:1, remember).

2. Consider ditching your bucket and spade. Yet another scientific survey suggests that 'compaction' is key to building a sturdy castle and that hands are therefore better for the job than any other tools, since they can pat down the sand most effectively.

3. A wide base is key. More scientific research (honestly, I'm as surprised as you) suggests that a castle with a 2 cm (¾ in) radius can be 27 cm (11 in) tall before toppling, one with a 7 cm (3 in) radius could be 60 cm (24 in) tall, and a column with a 20 cm (8 in) radius could, theoretically, be an intimidating 2.5 m (8 ft) tall.

4. Don't forget your imagination. The best sandcastles aren't the tallest, most compact or most perfect ones. They're the weird, wobbly, wonky ones, bedecked in shells and seaweed and encircled in myriad moats. Go for it.

Older children Why stop at a castle? They can make a whole city.

Toddlers might still find a traditional bucket and spade easier and faster.

DIG TO AUSTRALIA

Or, if you are reading this Down Under, then dig to the UK, or the centre of the Earth. Dig an *enormous* hole, basically. As big and as deep as you can. Then try not to fall into it.

CREATE A SHELL MONSTER

Legend is chockablock with sea monsters, from the aspidochelone (a giant turtle that lures sailors to their doom) to the Iku-Turso (variously described as an enormous octopus or walrus) via the Scylla (six heads, twelve legs, a bit scary…). Here's how to make your own.

1. Hunt for shells of different shapes and sizes. Mussel shells make good bodies, cockles can be heads, scallops make lovely skirts, razor shells are ideal arms and legs.

2. When you've collected all your shells, experiment with arranging them into different monsters.

3. Don't forget that seaweed can make excellent hair.

BUILD A SAND SCULPTURE

Think outside the fortress and try sculpting a turtle, a mermaid, a pirate ship, a car to sit in, anything… The same principles apply: damp sand, regularly patted down so that it's nice and compact, and using a trowel for the digging and your hands for the finer work. Just remember that dunes are a fragile natural habitat.

BURY YOUR PARENTS

And parents, don't call me a traitor until you've considered this: it basically involves you *lying flat* – maybe even with a book – while the children potter extremely close by without straying, possibly for a span of minutes running into double figures.

1   Get a parent (or anyone, in fact) to lie flat in the sand.

2   Use a trowel (or plastic spade) to bury them in sand.

3   Pat down the sand as you cover them until there's a nice, thick, compacted layer of sand from their toes all the way to their collarbone – to make it as difficult as possible for them to escape.

HOLD A HOUDINI CONTEST

1   Choose your contestants (or aspiring escapologists), and dig a hole in the sand for each: they want to be knee deep in sand, so dig accordingly and remember that some holes will need to be deeper than others to account for varying heights.

2   Get each contestant to stand in their hole, then fill up the holes with damp sand, patting down as you go to make a good, compact jail for their legs.

3   Shout, 'On your marks, get set, GO!' and watch the contestants wriggle furiously in an attempt to escape. The first contestant to free their legs and climb out, wins.

Note You can either allow the use of arms for digging or not, but it's a much better spectator sport if you don't.

PAINT WITH SAND

1   Decide on the pattern or picture you're going to make.

2   Use a brush to draw onto your paper with glue.

3   Now shake sand all over the paper.

4   Pick up the paper and give it a very gentle shake. The sand will fall away from everywhere except the areas you've painted, leaving your picture revealed in sand.

WRITE A SECRET MESSAGE

1   Take a piece of white paper and write a secret message in glue.

2   Then tip sand over the whole paper, and give it a light shake to reveal the message.

CONSTRUCT A DAM

1 Find out the times of tidal movements in your area. You want to build as the tide is coming in, otherwise you'll get bored waiting for the waves and won't get to see how well your dam holds up against them.

2 Use a trowel (or spade) and your hands to build a big, semi-circular wall out of sand and pebbles. It wants to be tall, wide and compact in order to survive attack by the tide for as long as possible, and to curl away from the sea so that you can stand, protected, inside the curve of its C-shape for as long as possible.

3 Pat down the wall firmly as you build otherwise it will crumble fast.

4 Add rocks, pebbles, big shells – whatever you can find, really – to the base to strengthen the structure.

5 When it's as strong as you think it can be, wait for the tide to approach and see how long the wall withstands the pressure of the water before it collapses into the sea and you run squealing away.

PLAY NOUGHTS AND CROSSES IN THE SAND

1 Go hunting for some driftwood or twigs and some pebbles. You'll need at least eight lengths of driftwood or twigs (but they don't have to be big), and four pebbles or rocks (or shells, actually, since anything goes).

2 Use one of the twigs to draw a basic 'noughts-and-crosses' grid in the sand.

3 Nominate one person to be 'noughts' and give them the pebbles. Another person needs to be 'crosses', and they get the pieces of wood.

4 'Crosses' goes first. They place two bits of their wood in a cross on one of the squares of the grid.

5 Now 'noughts' gets to place a pebble in the square of their choice.

6 The first person to make a straight line across the grid with their beach materials is the winner, and gets to go first if you play again.

GO BEACHCOMBING

Be warned: beachcombing can be dangerous. Sharp objects aside, more than one child I've engaged in this activity has, afterwards, taken a disquieting interest in metal detectors...

1 Go down to the beach at low tide.

2 Walk along the water's edge, inspecting the sand carefully for treasure.

3 Gingerly lift up anything that looks like treasure: it could be a shell, a piece of driftwood, an interesting pebble, cockles or a piece of sea glass.

4 If an object seems safe to handle and interesting or beautiful enough to merit it, put it in your pocket or a bucket.

5 When you've combed your stretch of beach, empty your pockets and gloat over all your treasure.

Note Remember to leave some for nature. Don't strip the beach clean.

Toddlers The best of this treasure can be brought home and used as props for a nature or water table.

Older children can turn their treasure into a piece of art – a collage, maybe, or one of the following ideas....

MAKE A SHELL NECKLACE OR BRACELET

Have you noticed how many seashells have holes in them? Apparently, this is because Dog Whelks and Necklace Shells – among others – feed on other molluscs by 'drilling' a small hole through their shells and sucking out their insides. Sounds a bit grisly for a craft project? Well, that's nature – red in tooth and claw, but occasionally producing just the right conditions for pretty shell jewellery...

1   Comb the beach for shells with holes in them.

2   Cut a length of string that, when tied into a loop, will be able to fit over your head or on your wrist.

3   Thread your favourite shell (or shells) onto the string.

4   Tie together the ends of the string and wear your beachcombed baubles with pride.

Note Try using a length of beach grass instead of string.

MAKE A SHELL MOBILE (OR WIND CHIME)

1   Find a stick or piece of driftwood.

2   Decide how low you want your shells to hang, and cut several lengths of string accordingly (you might want some shells to hang lower than others).

3   Now tie one end of the string around a shell (or sea glass, or whatever), and the other to the stick.

4   Continue tying shells at different points in your lengths of string, remembering to balance their weight evenly across the mobile so that it hangs straight.

5   Cut one last piece of string, tying it to the centre of the stick at one end and making a loop at the other, from which to hang your mobile and display it.

Note You can use the same method to make a wind chime, with just a few changes. You'll need two sticks to start with. Arrange them into a cross and tie them at the middle. Cut four lengths of string (a good hand-span longer than you want your finished mobile to hang). Tie shells at regular intervals along each length of string. Now hang a length of string from each point of your cross. Create a loop of string at the centre of the cross so you can hang your chimes in the wind, and wait for the shells to knock against each other.

LISTEN TO THE SEA

I've never felt more like a magician than the first time I held a shell to my child's ear and saw his pupils dilate with wonder. It didn't last long, but it felt incredible, as though I was briefly channelling the magic of generations through that one, familiar gesture.

1   Walk the beach to find a large, empty shell.

2   Put its concave side up to your ear.

3   Listen: can you hear the sea? It's as if the whole ocean is contained inside this one shell.

For older children Why do shells make this noise? Scientists believe that what you're actually hearing is an echo of the 'ambient' or background noise that's all around you. When it travels into the shell it resonates around it, creating the eerie 'ocean' sound you hear.

DISCOVER A MOLLUSC 'S AGE

Here's a thing we learnt recently that genuinely astonished me: most bivalves (molluscs with two shells, so that's clams, oysters, mussels, scallops and so on to you and me) have growth rings on their shells, just like you see on felled tree trunks.

It works like this: the shells are made, mostly, from *calcium carbonate*, extracted from the surrounding water. Over time layers of calcium are built up around the outer edges, so that the shell gets wider, longer and thicker. So:

1   Look at a bivalve shell and you'll see a series of concentric, curved lines on it – each of these represents the layer of shell, or calcium carbonate, put down in one growing season.

2   Count the number of rings, and it's thought you have a rough estimate of its age. Amazing, no?

TREES

Now don't get me wrong, I love a good playground. Our local one is a godsend, a miracle in multicoloured play equipment. Without it, we'd watch approximately 5,000 times more TV. Because of it, we are outdoors everyday, jostling for our place in a swirling tornado of small feet stomping on Astroturf, small hands grasping metal poles, small bodies rolling down landscaped surfaces and swinging from synthetic ropes.

We are outdoors and in a park, but rarely touch anything in any way, well, natural. Why, I started to wonder, are all the trees and grass on the other side of the fence?

It was around then that I stumbled across an article by Tim Gill, one of the UK's leading thinkers on childhood, in *The Guardian* newspaper. It was an ode to tree climbing. 'Working out how to start,' he wrote, 'testing for strength, feeling how the breeze in your face also sways the branches underfoot, glimpsing the changing vista through the leaves, dreaming about being king or queen of the jungle, shouting to your friends below once you've got as high as you dare – is an immersive, 360-degree experience that virtual or indoor settings simply cannot compare with.'

But how does playground equipment compare? To find out, we went to see Tim. While Johnny poked intently into the depths of Tim's garden pond with a stick, Tim explained that European standards for playgrounds state that: 'the inclination of stairs shall be constant... the treads shall be spaced equally, stairs shall be of uniform construction, and shall be horizontal within 3°.'

Wonkiness – the definitive characteristic of trees – is, in effect, discouraged. And if that minimises the risk to our kids, that must be a good thing... right?

Well the first question is, does it really? In 2002, a detailed, strategic risk assessment of British playgrounds was made by Professor J. Ball, for the Health and Safety Executive. It concluded that, despite the many modifications made to the country's playgrounds in the name of safety over the last decade, admissions to Accident and Emergency that were connected to them had remained pretty much constant since the Eighties.

Professor Bell suggested that, counterintuitively, children might actually take more risks in an apparently safe environment than they do in one where it's obvious they ought to keep their wits about them.

His report put the average annual number of childhood visits to A&E that are connected to public playground equipment at just over 21,000. Meanwhile, in 2006, only 1,163 under fifteens were admitted to hospital suffering injuries relating to falls from trees. And just put that in context, within the same period, 2,365 under fourteens were injured in falls from beds.

Of course, those low figures for tree-climbing are partly down to the smaller number of kids climbing up and into them in the first place. In 2010 a third of the children aged between six and eleven who took part in a Play England survey had never climbed a tree. But I can't help wondering whether more children might be falling off chairs and out of bed *because* they aren't climbing trees.

Back in 2002, Professor Bell pointed out the difficulty of balancing the dangers of exposing our children to small amounts of risk (injury, lawsuits...) against the potential benefits (physical, social and psychological development).

Then, in 2011, a study found that British ten-year-olds had less muscular strength and a weaker grip than children who had been born a decade before, because they played indoors instead of up trees. In another ten years' time, will our kids have to wear bubble-wrap suits just to eat a sandwich in safety? Give me a small tumble from a tree, any day.

FACTS TO FIRE THE IMAGINATION

- In a year, an acre of trees is thought to absorb as much carbon as is produced by driving a car for 14,000 km (8,700 miles), and produces the same amount of oxygen as is consumed by 18 people.
- In 2004, scientists discovered the world's oldest tree on a Swedish mountain. The Norwegian Spruce was estimated to be 9,550 years old, dating back to the end of the last ice age.
- The world's tallest tree is a Coast Redwood in California that measures more than 110 m (360 ft) in height.
- 'Moon trees' were grown from seeds that circled the moon 34 times in *Apollo 14* astronaut Stuart Roosa's pocket in 1971. The idea was to see what effect weightlessness had on growth. One was planted at the White House.
- An oak, when attacked by insects, releases poisonous tannin as a gas.
- Ancient Greek physicians used willow to treat fever, earache, gout, dandruff and gas. In 1899 salicylic acid, extracted from willow bark, was synthesised to produce asprin.

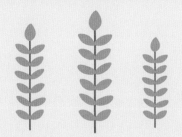

TOOLKIT TO TAKE

Scissors
Paper
PVA glue
Brush
Needle and thread
Pencil
Paint
Crayons
White cotton fabric
Measuring tape
String
Magnifying glass
Sellotape
Jam jar
Card
Optional extra: a family photo

IDEAS TO START WITH

MAKE LEAF BUNTING

A friend and I came up with this natural (and free) decoration for her daughter's summer birthday party, then realised that the making of it made a great party activity, too.

1   Go hunting for fallen leaves – as many different shapes and sizes as possible.

2   Cut a long length of string.

3   Use a pencil to carefully pierce holes in the tops of the leaves.

4   Thread the string through the holes so that the leaves are hanging from it.

5   Tidy up your bunting, so that the leaves are equally spaced (or arranged however you like them).

6   Hang the bunting between trees, or indoors if you prefer.

Note You can paint your leaves too, or turn the bunting into a 'Wishing Tree' by getting the kids to write a wish on their leaf before stringing up each one.

MAKE A TREE COLLAGE

Even health and safety monitors couldn't object to these tiny imitations. Try adding twig hedges, bushes, fences or even scarecrows to the scene too.

1   Head out to look for twigs. You need one larger one to make your mini tree's trunk, and a bunch of smaller ones to make its branches.

2   Now look for little leaves. Hedges are sometimes better than trees if you want to find leaves that look the right size for your mini tree.

3   Glue your 'tree trunk' onto a piece of paper.

4   Arrange the smaller twigs and leaves around the top of the trunk, to make a convincing tree-top.

5   When you're happy with the arrangement, glue the elements into place.

6   Display on the fridge, or give it to an adoring relative for theirs.

Note Use Sellotape if your branches resist sticking to the paper.

MAKE A LEAF COSTUME

It's lovely to make a costume for a fairy. Sadly, my companions usually focus on leaf 'armour' for knights, weapons for superheroes and camouflage for ninjas.

1   Use crayons to draw the character of your choice on a piece of paper (nice and big so that you can decorate it).

2   Think about what kind of clothes your character needs and what shapes of leaves you might need in order to make them (two Sycamore leaves might make good wings for a fairy, two Ash leaves make a good eye-mask for a ninja, a bunch of Rowan leaves could make a great tutu, and a really good maple leaf makes a dress with two arms at the top and the body below).

3   Go out to look for your leaves, bring them back and experiment with laying them over your character to make clothes.

4   When you're happy, stick them on using a brush and glue.

5   Voila! A fairy! (Or a ninja...)

Note You can do this with a photo, too. Use one of your family or friends, and give them a makeover by gluing leaf skirts, shirts, shoes and wings to it. It makes a good gift and if you paint the leaves in PVA glue they'll last longer.

MAKE A LEAF MASK

Of course, if you'd rather *be* a character than dress one up, you can always use your leaves to make yourself a mask.

1   Cut out the shape of the mask from coloured paper or card, remembering to make holes for eyes. The bigger the mask, the thicker your paper will need to be.

2   Find leaves in suitable colours and shapes for your design.

3   Arrange the leaves on top of the mask in the design of your choosing. Remember that they can stick out well beyond the edges of the paper in all directions, but mustn't cover the eyeholes.

4   Glue them down in the pattern you've chosen.

5   When dry, use a stick or pencil to push a hole through each side of the mask. Tie a generous length of string to each end.

6   Hold the mask to your face and tie the string round the back of your head. Go out and adventure, in character.

Toddlers will need grown-ups to get involved at the cutting stage.

MAKE A LEAF CROWN

This uses the same method as daisy-chain making, but with leaves. Obviously.

1   Find a nice pile of big leaves with their stems intact. Sycamore and maple work best and you want ones with quite long stems attached.

2   Cut the ends of the stems at a sharp angle.

3   Take the first leaf and fold it in half (along the rib that runs from the stem, down its middle to its tip).

4   Do the same to a second leaf.

5   Place the two leaves along an imaginary horizontal line: one in front of the other, with their stems pointing in the same direction.

6   Use the stem of one leaf to push holes through the other leaf, weaving in and out of its folded sides.

7   The leaves should now be joined together.

8   Take another leaf, fold it in half in the same way, and thread its stem through the first leaf.

9   Carry on until you have a chain big enough to wrap around your head.

10 Now connect the two ends in the same way (or use Sellotape if you're a cheat!).

Toddlers might prefer to cut out a crown of paper and attach leaves to it with glue or double-sided tape, as this is really quite a fiddle.

TRY THE TREE 'YOGA' POSE

1   Stand somewhere peaceful with your feet together and your hands by your sides.

2   Shift your weight to your left foot.

3   Focus on a steady object in front of you (it will help you balance).

4   Bend your right knee and use your hand to draw up your right foot, so you can press its sole against the inside of your left thigh, toes pointing down to the floor, knees out to the side.

5   Put your hands on your hips, then reach them up to the sky.

MEASURE A TREE'S HEIGHT

1   Choose a tree.

2   Walk away from it in a straight line, pausing regularly to bend right over and look back at it from between your legs.

3   Keep walking until you can just about see the top of the tree from between your legs.

4   Mark the spot, or get someone else to stand there while you...

5   Use a tape measure to measure the distance from the tree to your spot.

6   Whatever measurement you have – that's (roughly) the height of the tree.

Older children Explain that the reason this works is that if you view a tree's top at a 45-degree angle, the height of the tree is equivalent to the distance you are from it.

MAKE A NATURE PRINT

A good one for a long, sunny day in the garden.

1   Go out and find leaves in lots of different, interesting shapes.

2   Wet a piece of fabric, give it a squeeze, then lay it flat in a place that will remain in the sun for several hours.

3   Mix your paints with roughly the same amount of water.

4   Paint the fabric in colourful patterns or blocks.

5   Press your leaves gently into the painted fabric, in whatever pattern you like. Make sure you've pressed their edges down (you may want to put pebbles on top of them to hold them down).

6   Leave the fabric out in the sun until it is completely dry. This will take a few hours.

7   Now peel off the leaves. You should be left with pale leaf shapes all over your brightly coloured fabric.

FIGURE OUT THE AGE OF A TREE

For those who are more 'small Sherlock Holmes' than 'mini Martha Stewart'.

1   Select a tree, any tree.

2   At about 'child's head height', or 1.2 m (4 ft), wrap a measuring tape around the tree's trunk.

3   Take a note of the measurement in centimetres.

4   Divide the result by 2.5. The number you arrive at should be a rough estimate of the tree's age.

Note This is not an exact science as the speed at which trees grow varies according to things like their species and location.

DO SOME BARK RUBBING

When we first started spending more and more time outdoors, we got our fair share of gentle 'hippy' jibes. I promise, though, this is the closest we've come to hugging a tree. And even some of the most determined dirt dodgers have now begrudgingly given it their approval.

1   Find a tree with good bark – an interesting pattern perhaps, deep grooves, whatever you like.

2   Hold up a piece of paper against the tree.

3   Rub a crayon all over the paper until you can see the pattern of the bark on the paper (you may want to peel off the crayon's label and roll it lengthways along the sheet).

4   Now try another tree and see how the pattern it produces is different, or try creating a patchwork of different bark patterns and different colours on a single piece of paper.

MAKE A BARK PHOTO FRAME

Discarded bark is good for making all sorts of stuff, especially hand-made birthday presents.

1   Find a family photo in which the action is centred in the middle and the outer edges of the photo are unimportant.

2   Find some strips of fallen bark and arrange them into a frame around the photo's edges.

3   Glue everything in place and weigh it all down under a book until it's dry.

4   Tada! A speedy, free (and, of course, thoughtful) gift.

BUILD A FAIRY HOUSE

A bit fiddly, this, so not one for toddlers to take on. But with patience older children can make something really quite beautiful.

1   Find the longest, thickest strip of bark you can.

2   Soak it in water overnight or until it bends easily in your fingers (you could be in for a bit of a wait).

3   Find the middle and cut a little arch into it with scissors – this will be your door.

4   Wrap the bark around a jam jar (ideally, you want it to stretch right round and overlap a little, but you can use two separate pieces if yours aren't wide enough).

5   Cut a few lengths of string and tie them around the jar, holding the bark securely in place.

6   Leave overnight.

7   Untie the string, take off the curled bark from the jam jar, and glue its ends together so that it forms a loo roll shape.

8   Now you have curved walls of your house, you just need to make the roof. For this you can use other sheets of bark, twigs, moss or flowers.

CONDUCT A MINIBEAST HUNT IN DEAD WOOD

. . . .

Take a magnifying glass to a pile of dead wood or curls of discarded bark. Which minibeasts can you find?

MAKE A BARK MONSTER

Since trees are bumpy and covered in branches, some bark you find discarded has holes in it. These, we discovered, make excellent eyes...

1 Find a piece of bark with a hole in it.

2 Imagine that this hole is an eye. The shape of the bark and the position of the hole in it will determine what kind of creature you turn it into.

3 If the bark is long and thin, you might make a crocodile's face in profile, by cutting or painting two rows of teeth or a pair of red lips onto it.

4 If the piece of bark is more of an oval, you could try cutting it into the shape of a fish in profile, with one eye peering out. The world is your oyster (though oysters are actually one of a minority of creatures that don't have any eyes to speak of).

BUILD A LOG-PILE HOME FOR ANIMALS

A pile of dead wood and bark. It might not seem much to you, but when you're outdoors, you need to change the way you look at things. Because to some creatures, that pile is, well, a country pile. A mansion of the utmost luxury. To yet more, it's a gluttonous, ten-course banquet. And since wood piles are increasingly rare, why not do a critter a kindness and build one?

1 Collect an assortment of different kinds of wood, twigs, branches and different-sized logs with the bark on.

2 Find a spot with dappled shade falling on it (bright sun will dry out the logs, but total shadow might be too cold for some insects).

3 Pile up the wood.

4 That's it. Just keep an eye out for mosses, fungi and insects making their homes there, and birds coming to feed off them.

FEATHERS

Feathers have always been treasured: by the theropod dinosaurs whose ancient bodies were covered in them; by the Mayan priests in ancient Central America who worked them into broad-rimmed hats; by the English aristocrats of the Middle Ages who decorated their head-dresses with them; by the scribes who penned the Magna Carta with them and, later, by those who wrote up the American Declaration of Independence using them; by Jane Austen who wrote her novels with one; by children who snuggled down under quilts stuffed with them; by penguins that use them to keep dry, seabirds that use them to keep waterproof and peacocks that use them to impress; by flamingos that extract pigments from algae and brine shrimp to make theirs pink; and by the kingfishers whose feathers are made blue by the way their feathers interact with light.

And now they are treasured by us, as we stomp the streets and local parks in the late summer, picking them up as we go and stuffing them into bags and pockets.

Towards the end of the season, lots of birds have finished mating and there's no need to impress the opposite sex or each other with posh plumage. So by the final, butter-coloured days of late summer, feathers are being moulted and are floating down onto pavements, into gardens and across playgrounds. It's the avian equivalent of packing away your flashy beachwear and slumping back into your favourite, forgiving jumper with a packet of biscuits.

So for us, feathers seem symbolic of a wider change in the air: of evenings folding in and the summer clothes folded up; of the first hints of the curling up of creatures and curling round of scarves, the fire draining from the sun and settling its blood-orange hues onto leaves instead.

The end of one chapter, and the beginning of the next.

FACTS TO FIRE THE IMAGINATION

- Some experts think that feathers evolved from scales, which most birds still have on their legs and feet.
- Most birds have an annual moult, when old feathers drop out and new ones grow. It can take from four to 16 or more weeks.
- Birds spend a huge amount of time using their beaks to preen and clean their feathers. Some vultures fly up to 32 km (20 miles) to find the water they need to bathe their feathers in.
- The lowest recorded number of feathers on a songbird is 940 on a hummingbird, while the highest - 25,216 - was recorded on a swan. Most songbirds have between 1,500 and 3,000.

TOOLKIT TO TAKE

Scissors
Magnifying glass
Paper
Sellotape
PVA glue
Crayons
Needle and thread
Card
String
Blu-tack
Crayons
Pencils
Jam jar
Double-sided sticky tape
Paints and brush
Ribbons

IDEAS TO START WITH

MAKE A BIRD MASK

Is it a bird? Is it a plane? Or maybe it's a bionic superhero hybrid of the two? You can make this feather-covered mask into whatever weird or wonderful thing is occupying your imagination today.

1   Draw the shape of your mask onto a piece of card.

2   Hold it against your face, then gently press a crayon against the places where your eyes are. Now you can cut eyeholes around the crayon mark.

3   Go hunting for feathers. If you want to cover the whole mask and make your disguise convincing, you'll need lots. Consider using different lengths, too – short, fluffy ones in the middle of the mask and a longer fringe around the edges?

4   Now cover your mask in a layer of PVA glue and stick the feathers onto it. Longer feathers will need their shafts daubed in glue, too.

5   When it's dry, carefully push a pencil through each side to make holes and tie a length of sting to each. Now you can tie them together behind your head.

6   See if you can con the birds into conversing with you

Toddlers are going to need help with the cutting, but will love the messy gluing bit.

MAKE A FEATHER COLLAGE

1   Go on a feather hunt.

2   Empty your pockets onto the ground and see what shapes you can make with them. It could be an abstract masterpiece. Otherwise individual feathers can make excellent limbs, hairstyles, squirrel tails or surfboards. Collections of feathers are ideal for clouds, snowy hillsides, the surf of waves and, yes, birds themselves.

3   On paper draw or paint the other shapes or details you want to include.

4   Now brush glue on the areas where you want to add feathers.

5   Press feathers into the glue, then wait for it to dry and reveal your masterpiece.

MAKE A NATIVE AMERICAN FEATHER HEADBAND

The famous feather head-dresses worn by the Sioux tribe of North America were a finickity business. First, each feather had to be earned by an act of great bravery. Then, only tail feathers of the Golden Eagle would do, which usually meant capturing a young eagle from its nest and waiting until it reached maturity before plucking the tail feathers.

The tribes of the north-east woodlands, on the other hand, were less choosy. Their headbands could be made from bunches of other feathers, including those of turkeys, hawks, egrets and cranes. Since stealing, then raising a Golden Eagle is an illegal and ethically dubious endeavour, here are the instructions for making the latter.

1   Cut card into long strips of equal width.

2   Sellotape a couple together and bend them around your head to check the length you'll need for your headband. Cut it accordingly.

3   Now you can paint patterns onto the headband.

4   While you're waiting for it to dry, hunt for some feathers. Long ones are ideal.

5   Turn over the headband and use lengths of sellotape to stick the feathers onto the back. You want them to stand up high above the top of the headband when it is flipped over, but they might not balance for long unless you secure their bases towards the bottom of the headband.

6   Stand the headband up, bend it into a loop and stick together the overlapping ends with Sellotape. Done!

Toddlers might need help with the cutting.

GO ON A FEATHER HUNT

Our haul is usually pretty heavy in pigeon feathers. But not always. Sometimes we find gems. See how many different kinds of feather you can find in one outing.

DRAW A FEATHER

So you've found a common or garden pigeon feather. It may not be a peacock plume, but all feathers have beautiful textures and subtle shading in them, which you'll see if if you look closely. Trying to draw one can be amazingly absorbing, almost meditative, if you're that way inclined.

1   Find some feathers.

2   Examine each feather carefully through a magnifying glass. Look for the details you wouldn't otherwise notice. Is it feather fluffy at the bottom and glossy at the top? Does the intensity of its colour alter as it travels up? Are its edges smooth or jagged?

3   Now try to draw the feathers, replicating all the things that make them unique.

MAKE FEATHER JEWELLERY

If you've collected a good hoard of feathers and have a few that aren't too ragged, have a go at making some jewellery out of the best ones. Try pushing a needle and thread through the thickest part of the shafts without splitting them, so that the feathers hang off the thread. When you've threaded enough onto the cotton, tie the ends together and you've got a bracelet, necklace or (if you hang the loop over an ear) an earring.

Otherwise, cut out a length of card to make a chunkier bracelet. Paint it, then glue feathers onto it before sticking the two ends together with Sellotape to make a cuff that slips over your hand and onto your wrist.

Toddlers can use double-sided sticky tape to stick feathers to a cardboard version if you want to save on time and mess.

Older children can use brightly coloured cotton or ribbon to make a more eye-catching bracelet.

MAKE A QUILL PEN

The word pen comes from the Latin word *penna*, which means feather. A decent proportion of the most important documents in Western civilisation were written with a quill pen. I'm not saying you'll end up making history if you make your own quill pen, but the chances are greater that you will do so.

1   Go out to find the perfect feather. It will be long enough to hold comfortably, with a thick and sturdy shaft.

2   Trim the sides of the feather at the bottom for a better grip.

3   With a pair of sharp scissors, very carefully cut the bottom of the shaft at a 45-degree angle. Don't worry if it doesn't work first time – keep trying.

4   Clean out the materials left inside the shaft with the end of your scissors or a needle.

5   Water down some paint a little, until it's the consistency of ink.

6   Now dip your quill pen into the paint and use it to write something of historic importance on paper. No pressure.

Toddlers The making of the pen is a bit fiddly for them, but they can join in with the writing and drawing once it's made.

AUTUMN

The poet T. S. Eliot had April down as the cruellest month, but he was, sadly, mistaken. In Britain, at least, it's September. Given the choice I would happily hibernate through the transition from summer to autumn, and miss out on the dispiriting drawing in of the evenings, the glum greying of the skies and soddening of all surfaces, which seem to bring with them a spike in moaning from the minors in the family (and, possibly, the majors, too).

It's in these months that our guilty secrets, our latent addictions to TV and tablets (tablet *computers*, that is – things aren't quite that bad, even in autumn) stop being, well… secret. We let it all hang out. We breakfast with *Fireman Sam*, lunch with *Thomas the Tank Engine* and are quite often still to be found in our pyjamas, covered in crumbs, by tea time (which we take with *Tree Fu Tom*).

Now roll up a copy of *Perfect Parenting Magazine* and smack me over the knuckles with it if you want, but I think telly gets a bad rap. My kids have learnt loads from the box, and not just how to get Netflix up and running in under 30 seconds. They've emerged from viewings with startling new vocabulary and facts about everything from the deep sea to deep space.

On the other hand, intense doses do, demonstrably, turn them into square-eyed zombies. After a couple of days of heavy viewing they still *look* like human children. Gaze into their glazed pupils, however, and it's immediately clear they are, in fact, monsters, devoid of independent thought and – when forcibly prized from the sofa – capable only of raging about the house, tearing it apart in their hunt for the remote control and their next screen fix. It's striking how fast this possession occurs. Their attention span shrinks, their ability to think outside the (TV) box shrivels, and their irritability swells like a tidal wave to come crashing down on the nearest parental figure.

And so, for the sake of everybody's sanity – we try to get out. It hasn't always been easy. If this were an Oscars' speech, our tearful list of thank-yous would extend to fleeces, warm socks, wellies, waterproofs, hot chocolate in flasks, snacks and bribes … we couldn't have done it without any of them.

It's always worth it, though. Nature, I'll admit, is a far subtler teacher than the telly. Accidentally, without realising it, kids and adults alike find themselves learning.Counting and sorting acorns, weaving stories around unwitting earthworms, balancing on wet, wobbly branches, weighing, measuring, stretching, running, building, making and negotiating with each other along with the terrain. We find focus wriggling among the woodlice and worms under wet logs. The calm of the rooted trees is shared out across their rain-pooled leaves. Pent-up energy dissipates into the gentle drizzle and is spread softly over the landscape.

Except for the times when a welly gets stuck in the mud. Hell hath no fury like a toddler who suddenly finds one socked foot wobbling precariously over a muddy puddle.

FACT BOX

- The average British child watches almost 2½ hours of TV a day. That's over 17 hours a week. The figure has risen by 12 per cent since 2007.
- Britain's 11–15-year-olds are so addicted to their electronic devices that they spend 7½ hours a day in front of a screen – an increase of 40 per cent in a decade and around half their waking lives.
- Scores in creativity tests are improved by 50 per cent after people spend four days backpacking, disconnected from electronic devices, according to a 2012 study by the Universities of Utah and Kansas.
- In 2005, the American Institutes for Research found that learning in nature significantly improved children's scores in science, language, arts and maths. Outdoor science programmes, for instance, increased test scores by 27 per cent.
- The Wilderness Foundation UK, which takes troubled teenagers into the mountains, has found that their behaviour, self-control and self-awareness all improved.
- A 2008 report by Britain's schools inspection body, Ofsted, points out that learning outside raises 'standards, motivation, personal development and behaviour, can help to make subjects more vivid and interesting for pupils and enhance their understanding ... and could make an important contribution to pupils' future economic wellbeing.'
- A 2000 study measuring children's ability to focus and think found their cognitive abilities increased when they had views of, and daily exposure to, natural settings.

ACORNS, CONKERS AND PINE CONES

'I think we'd all concede that something has gone seriously wrong with the spirit of health and safety in the past decade. When children are made to wear goggles by their headteacher to play conkers … When village fêtes are cancelled because residents can't face jumping through all the bureaucratic hoops …'

That was British Prime Minister David Cameron, back in 2009, in a speech to the Policy Exchange think-tank. And yeah, he may have been hamming it up for the hordes, but by 2011 almost one in six teachers said their schools now outlawed games of conkers in case of injury by Horse Chestnut.

So here we are, in high-vis vests, Taking a Stand. It may not be a village fete, but we've jumped through the hoops to get our road closed to traffic for two hours in order for local children to be able to play outside. We have tea and trestle tables, and the neighbours have made samosas. Someone from the council has turned up with a ping-pong table. And there are conkers, pine cones and acorns.

The first recorded game of conkers – using the now-traditional seeds of the Horse Chestnut tree – dates back to 1848 on the Isle of Wight, but the same game was played, even earlier than that, with hazelnuts or cobnuts, or even snail shells.

Can it be really true that children can no longer be trusted to play this historic game without losing an eye? That their parents can't be trusted to take the risk without launching legal action?

More widely, is it true that children have forgotten how to play on their own, without the help of screens, plastics and flashing lights? Will they even come outside in the cold? We are about to find out.

Half an hour later, I do a headcount. There are 150 people on our road. 150 different faces representing almost as many colours and ages, backgrounds, religious practices, languages, stories, private lives, hopes and fears. Two simple things have brought them together: samosas and the novelty of being able to stand in the road without risking death by engine or exhaust.

A couple of kids are using chalk to draw around leaves on the pavement. Some more have sketched a wobbly finishing line across the road and are hurtling towards it on bikes and scooters. Someone sits on the kerb, picking the scales from a pine cone with intense concentration. On a corner, a game of conkers kicks off while a small figure falls from his bike, is peeled off the road by a stranger and careers off again, grinning.

Nobody looses an eye. Nobody sues anybody else. The adults eat cake and brush samosa crumbs from their coats, and meet each other's eyes with the same look. It's a look that is at once bemused and happy. It says, 'Oh look, who knew? Our children aren't crazed technology junkies. They are just… children. Like every generation before. And neither are we strangers, twitching at curtains, poised to steal each other's parking places, bins, children and samosas. We look quite different to each other but we are, actually… the same. We want the same things, kids and adults alike. And it's all really very simple, when it comes down to it: a safe, friendly and pleasant place to live, play and relax. How did it all get so complicated when the truth is, we are all, basically, just… nice?'

FACTS TO FIRE THE IMAGINATION

- An oak tree doesn't usually produce a large crop of acorns until it is 40 or 50 years old.
- Every few years English Oaks have a mast year, or a bumper crop of up to 50,000 acorns.
- The Coulter Pine, native to southern California, produces the heaviest pine cones in the world, weighing in at around 4.5 kg (10 lb) each, the same as a three-month old baby.
- Conkers are thought to have got their name form the French word *cogner*, meaning to hit.

TOOLKIT TO TAKE

Skewer
String
Paint
Brush
Scissors
Blu-tack
PVA glue
Paper
Jam jar
Crayons
Needle and thread
Trowel
Marker pen
Sellotape
Optional extra: peanut butter and either
   birdseed or muesli, if you have it lying around

IDEAS TO START WITH

MAKE ACORN NECKLACES

. . . .

For the mini fashionistas....

1   Go on an acorn hunt. You need soft green ones, as the hard brown ones are almost impossible to drive a needle through. Stop when you have enough for a necklace.

2   Thread a needle (doubling up the cotton), knot the end a couple of times and fold a square of Sellotape over it to stop acorns from sliding off later.

3   Push the needle carefully through an acorn.

4   Keep adding acorns, and tying knots between them to keep them in place, until you have enough to make a chunky necklace that will slip over your head.

5   Then cut the thread off the needle, remove the Sellotape and knot both ends of the thread together.

6   Wear the necklace, and watch it turn brown over time.

Toddlers will probably need quite a bit of help with the needle. They might prefer to make bracelets.

BE A SQUIRREL

. . . .

Otherwise known as turning a boring walk into a brilliant adventure.

1   Find some acorns.

2   Now find a good spot to bury them. Dig a hole with a trowel, then cover up the acorns. Take a good look at their location. Try to remember exactly where it is.

3   Now go for a walk. It has to be a long walk, with lots of twists and turns so that it's a proper challenge when you get back and...

4   Try to remember where you left the acorns. Can you find them and dig them up like a proper squirrel?

USE ACORN CAPS

To make a finger hat
Draw a little face on your fingertip. Then put the acorn cap over the top. Voila! A little man in a hat!

To make a fairy tea set
Pour a little puddle water into some acorn caps and you have 'tea' in 'tea cups' for a 'tea party' of fairies. Put some grass cuttings inside another acorn cap and they have a bowl of snacks to nibble on.

To make a whistle
1　Hold together the thumbs of both hands, nails facing one another. Then bend their knuckles ever so slightly so that a little triangle of space appears between the nails.

2　Hold the acorn cap in this space, supporting its back with your forefingers. Place your lower lip against the knuckles of your thumb, the upper lip sitting on top. Now blow hard! Yeah, I know – it's difficult. Keep trying.

MAKE AN AUTUMN CORSAGE

Or buttonhole. It's a buttonhole, really. But if you're in the company of someone who's into that whole American princess, prom-queen vibe then, we have learnt from bitter experience, 'corsage' might spark the imagination more effectively. Even if it makes you want to scream silently inside your own skull.

1　Head out for a walk, collecting, as you go, things that you think have interesting colours, textures or shapes to add to your corsage (buttonhole, ahem...).

2　Double up some thread on a needle, leaving it long enough to make a generous loop later.

3　Pushing the needle carefully through each of your finds, slide them all onto the cotton.

4　Snip the cotton from the needle and tie it carefully around your treasure, so that your finds are bunched neatly together at their ends.

5　Push their gathered ends into the buttonhole of a coat or shirt. Voila! A corsage (BUTTONHOLE).

FIND AN ACORN AND PLANT IT

Sometimes, the simplest things are the best.

1 Find an oak tree near your house. Keep it under surveillance, making regular trips to see it in the early autumn.

2 As soon as the tree's acorns start to drop, collect some (this needs to be done in this early stage).

3 Remove the caps from the acorns.

4 Pour some water into a jam jar, then drop your acorns into it.

5 Gather up the acorns that sink – these ones are good for planting.

6 Sow the acorns before they dry out. Dig 10 cm (4 in) into some earth outside, in several spaced out spots, drop in the acorns, then cover them gently. Or plant them singly in jam jars.

7 You should see some shoots in late April.

8 If you want to keep it in your garden plant it as far away as possible from your house, as they can grow very big. A better idea is to plant it in a pot in your garden and then later plant it somewhere with more space, like in school grounds.

BUILD AN ACORN MAN

... or an acorn lady, animal, monster, space buggy, spider... whatever your imaginations dictate.

1 Find four soft, green acorns – one for his head (ideally with its jaunty cap still attached), another for his body, and two for his feet – and a bunch of tiny fallen twigs that you can use for his legs, arms and neck.

2 Use your skewer to make two little holes at the base of one acorn. This acorn will be his body.

3 Snap two of your tiny twigs to the right length to make a pair of legs, and gently push their ends into the holes you've made.

4 Using the same method, make two little holes in the acorns destined to become his feet and push those onto the other ends of his legs.

5 Go back to the body acorn and make two little holes into which you can push his arms (once you've snapped twigs to the right lengths).

6 Now make the last hole on the top of his body and push a short twig into it to make his neck.

7 Make a hole in the acorn that's going to be his head, at the opposite end to the cap, and gently press this acorn onto the neck twig.

8 Now draw a little face on your man. You can even dress him up with leaves and flowers.

MAKE A CONKER MOBILE

1 Go out and collect as many conkers as you can, as well as two straightish sticks to make the frame of the mobile.

2 Arrange your sticks into a cross, and tie them firmly together in the middle of the cross.

3 Cut four lengths of string and tie the end of each to one arm of your stick frame

4 Adults should then use a skewer or corkscrew to pierce a hole right through each conker.

5 Now get the kids to thread the conkers onto the lengths of string, tying knots below them to keep them in place.

6 Cut one last piece of string. Tie one end round the middle of your frame and make a loop at the other end from which to hang your mobile.

7 Check to see you've weighted your mobile evenly (if it hangs wonkily, add more conkers to the lighter strings to even it out).

8 Hang it up and admire your work.

Note Thread pine cones in between the conkers for a different look.

MAKE A CONKER SNAKE OR CATERPILLAR

1 Go out and collect about eight conkers.

2 Using a skewer or corkscrew (and an adult), pierce a hole through the middle of each conker.

3 Now cut a length of string at least as long as your line of conkers.

4 Tie a knot in one end of the string, then thread your conkers onto it.

5 Knot the final end, and leave a little bit of thread after the knot – this will be your snake's tongue.

6 Use a marker pen to draw two eyes on the final conker.

7 Paint the excess length of string red to make a venomous tongue or add twigs for feelers.

MAKE A SECRET COMPARTMENT

1 Find a whole conker casing that has split, or is splitting, in two (you'll need both sides of it).

2 Remove the conker, if it's still in there.

3 Now you can keep small, secret things inside. Once you've deposited your treasure, try securing the two sides of the casing together with Blu-tack, but make sure it's not visible from the outside otherwise your secret will be blown.

MAKE A CONKER CREATURE

1 Find two conkers – one for your creature's head, one for its body – and a bunch of tiny twigs that you'll be able to use for legs, a neck, maybe even horns.

2 Your creature will stand on all-fours. To create its legs, pick a conker to be its body and use your skewer to make four little holes underneath it, like you're marking the corners of a square.

3 For the legs, get four twigs of equal length (or snap them to size), dab the end of each in glue and push the glued end into a hole. Now stand up your conker-body.

4 On the top surface of your conker make a hole to hold your creature's neck. Then snap a twig to the desired length, dab it in glue and push it into the hole.

5 Now make the head. Draw a little face on your second conker with a marker pen (the pale bit works best). Then make a hole with a skewer on its underneath and attach the head to the neck, dabbing the neck with glue first.

6 If you want to add horns, make one or two holes with your skewer on the top using the same method.

PLAY CONKERS

The rules of conker playing are so nuanced and hotly contested that setting down a definitive guide makes the Middle East peace process look like a game of tiddlywinks (probably also the subject of violent passions in certain, select circles). Here is an *extremely* simple guide. If you want to get more deeply involved, look online. But remember, you have been warned.

1 Find someone to play against.

2 Each player needs to find a conker.

3 Using a skewer or corkscrew (and an adult, if the players are young), pierce a hole through the centre of each conker.

4 Now cut a length of string, roughly from your elbow to your wrist.

5 Thread your conker onto the string, knotting it tightly at the end. Now you're ready to play.

6 Each player takes it in turn to hit the other's conker with their own, until one is destroyed.

7 Player one wraps her string around her hand, then lets the conker hang down, without moving, at arm's length.

8 Player two wraps his string around one hand, draws the conker up with his other hand, takes aim, then fires it at the opposing conker.

9 Now player one takes aim. The process is repeated, taking alternate turns, until one conker is decimated and the other claims victory

Note If you can't get your string through the conker, try wrapping a rectangle of Sellotape tightly around the end of it first.

MAKE A PINE-CONE CREATURE

Home-made by kids, these toys are huge in Scandinavia – literally so in Finland where there exists, apparently, a fairground boasting 'cone cow sculptures', cone creatures large enough for children to ride on. Lucky, lucky Finnish children…

1   Find a fallen pine cone.

2   Add legs to it by poking sticks between its scales.

3   Use a blade of glass or a leaf as a tail.

4   If the berries are out, squish a big one (blackberries are ideal) on to your creature's nose, and use smaller ones (elderberries for instance) for its eyes.

Older children can have a go at making other animals, too. A bird might have a twig beak and a couple of feathers for wings. A hedgehog perhaps needs pine needles as spikes. They could use sticks as horns or antlers, or moss to make a sheepy fleece.

DO SOME PINE-CONE PRINTING

Another firm favourite, involving as it does paint, and the opportunity to get it on any article of clothing and object that you have foolishly brought with you.

1 Collect pine cones.

2 Use a brush to paint the pine cones in various bright colours.

3 Roll the pine cones over paper to create patterns ('On the paper! I said PAPER!').

MAKE A WEATHER FORECASTER

Well, 'make' might be overstating things a bit. This has to be the easiest and simplest science project in history.

1 Find some pine cones.

2 Put a generous blob of Blu-tack on the base of each pine cone, and stick the pine cones on a window sill (outside).

3 Keep checking on your pine cones. When it's dry, they will open up. When it is going to rain, they will close. So you can put wellies on accordingly.

Older children Explain that the pine cones are really measuring humidity, not forecasting rain. When it's wet and humid, the scales swell up and the pine cone closes. This helps to protect the seeds, since they're spread by wind and might not travel very far in the rain. When it's dry, and they have a better chance of flying far and wide, the pine cone opens up, allowing the seeds to escape.

MAKE A GARLAND

1 Paint some pine cones (try making them multicoloured by painting the scales in different colours).

2 Once dry, cut a long length of string and, wrapping it tightly around the top scales, string your pine cones along it.

3 Hang the garland anywhere you desire.

PLAY PINE-CONE BOULES

This is a great Boxing Day game sparking the competitive streak in every generation in the family, from 70 year olds to 7 year olds, via the sofa-slumped teens.

1   Go out and collect pine cones – it's good to have four per player.

2   Find something else that's roundish to use as a marker – a conker or stone, perhaps.

3   Find a relatively flat bit of ground and decide on a starting line for all players to stand on.

4   Take turns to throw pine cones towards the marker – the closest pine cone wins!

Note You can also swap things around for a game of pine-cone bowling – find six big pine cones (or more), arrange them in rows, close together, then try knocking over as many as you can with a single throw of a conker. Or, play pine cone rounders using a pine cone as your ball and a stick as your bat.

MAKE CHRISTMAS DECORATIONS

I know, I know, I loathe the consumerist creep of Christmas too (It's OCTOBER! Why are you selling advent calendars?! Do you WANT me to cause grievous bodily harm to your display mannequins?!). But this activity is possibly the only time in which the words 'forward planning' can be justifiably used in the same sentence as 'fun'.

1   Paint some pine cones in many lurid and fluorescent colours (or tasteful gold and silver if you insist).

2   Attach each pine cone to a length of string.

3   Tie a loop at the other end of the string.

4   Forget about Christmas until December

And finally, if you have some spare peanut butter and birdseed (or muesli)...

MAKE A BIRDFEEDER

1   Wind some string around the top of a pine cone.

2   Tie a loop around the other end of the string, so you can hang it from a tree at the end.

3   Smear natural peanut butter thickly over the pine cone, then...

4   Roll it in birdseed or muesli.

5   Now hang the pine cone from a tree and wait for the birds to come.

Note Don't do this if you have a nut allergy. Obviously.

AUTUMN LEAVES

It's a well-documented fact that kids say the funniest things. Less frequently acknowledged, though, is the fact that the hilariously inventive thing stops being hilariously inventive somewhere around the millionth repetition. Also, when the thing they are saying, or the question they are asking, makes you look a bit, erm, stupid.

'Why do leaves change colour in autumn? Why? Why? WHYWHYWHYYYYYYYYYYYYYYY?'

'Well, the thing is...' It's a confident start, delivered as we stomp down the pavement, kicking the aforementioned leaves as we go. Like so many ill-fated explanations before it, however, it comes to an abrupt halt in much the same manner that my school-age concentration did during its scientific education.. 'The thing is...OH LOOK OVER THERE! A CONKER!'

Thank God for smart phones. 'So the thing IS,' I continue, scrolling manically through a Google search, 'The thing is, KEEP LOOKING OVER THERE! In the trees! AWAY from Mama when she's "thinking"! The thing is that in the summer, leaves turn water and carbon dioxide into oxygen and sugar through a process called PHO-TO-SYN-THES-IS. 'It's all very complicated, this photosynthesis, really you have to be extremely clever – yes, a bit like me – to understand. But basically, they use a chemical called chlorophyll to make photosynthesis happen and its chlorophyll that gives them their green colour.

'In the winter, there isn't enough light or water for photosynthesis to happen, so there's no need for the chlorophyll and it begins to fade from the leaves in autumn. That's why the green colour disappears and we start to see yellow and brown colours on the leaves. They've been there all along, you just haven't been able to see them in the summer because they've been covered up by the chlorophyll. At the same time, other magical processes are going on to add the brilliant red and burnished brown pigments we see in different kinds of leaves during autumn.'

'Woah! How amazing is that?! Johnny? Hello? Stop kicking those leaves. ARE YOU LISTENING?!' So here's another fact that should be better documented: the degree to which your kids' education is also a precious second chance to feel awe-inspired yourself.

FACTS TO FIRE THE IMAGINATION:

- Halloween is traditionally depicted in orange and black. Black to symbolise darkness and mystery, and orange because it is the colour of autumn leaves and pumpkins.
- Scientists believe global warming could significantly delay the process of leaves changing their colours.
- According to superstition, catching leaves in autumn brings good luck. Each leaf caught brings a lucky month next year.
- Fallen autumn leaves create a blanket of leaf litter on the ground that is home to creepy-crawlies. Millipedes eat rotting vegetation, while wood crickets feed on the leaves themselves as well as dead animals. Most of the minibeasts will die in their first winter.

TOOLKIT TO TAKE

PVA glue
Brush
Paper and card
Scissors
Sellotape
Double sided sticky tape
Jam jar
Needle and thread
Paints
Paper plate
Crayons
String
Candle
Pencil

IDEAS TO START WITH

MAKE LEAF STICK PUPPETS

. . . .

Because it's fun. And because your kids might be more amenable to a lecture on photosynthesis from Mr Leaf and the Fallen Foliage Crew than from you...

1   Go out and hunt for fallen autumn leaves. Find as many different shapes as possible.

2   Find some small sticks, too – you'll need the same number of these as you have of leaves.

3   Use some glue to stick the leaves onto paper, then cut them out (this just makes them a bit sturdier, later on).

4   Paint faces on the leaves.

5   Sellotape a stick to the back of each face.

6   Tada! A set of puppets. For educational purposes (possibly).

MAKE AN AUTUMN LEAF CROWN (WHILE YOU WALK)

. . . .

Or how to turn a conventional stroll into a colourful costume parade.

1   Cut out a crown from some paper, making sure it's the right length to fit around your own head.

2   Before you stick the ends together, stick at least one strip of double-sided sticky tape all the way along its length (two if you want to be ambitious).

3   Now use Sellotape to stick the ends together, put the crown on your head and set out on a walk.

4   As you walk collect autumn leaves, adding your favourites to the crown as you go by pressing them against the double-sided sticky tape.

MAKE A LEAF LANTERN

. . . .

This gives out a really calm orange glow...

1   Collect some autumn leaves. Think about the shapes they'll make when you glue them to a jam jar, and how you might arrange them.

2   Give the jam jar a good coat of PVA glue all over.

3   Stick your leaves on, in whatever pattern you want.

4   Leave for a while, coming back every now and again to push your leaves back down against the jar if they're curling up. Then paint over the whole surface with more PVA.

5   Once dried you've got your lantern! All you need do is to stick a candle inside and light it.

Note These make good Halloween decorations around the home and garden.

COLOUR SORTING

One for the toddlers, this.

1   Take four sheets of coloured paper. You need green, orange, brown and red (if you don't have these colours, you can always paint some white paper).

2   Lay out the paper on the ground and ask your small people to find leaves in matching colours, and to lay them in piles on the right sheets of paper.

3   Watch them spin, run and trip around wildly.

CAMOUFLAGE YOURSELF

Sometimes your kids need to go incognito among the woodland beasts. It's not a tidy business, and it may not be particularly pretty or parent-friendly. But when you're on an urgent, top-secret superhero mission, you just can't worry too much about that.

1   Wind double-sided sticky tape around your trouser legs, arms and body. You may need several strips on each limb.

2   Take off the protective backing so that the tape's outer face is sticky, too.

3   Now stick as many autumn leaves to yourself as you can. Try rolling in leaf piles and see what sticks to you. Or arrange leaves more artfully. It's up to you.

4   Now blend seamlessly into your environment, like a woodland ninja.

MATCH FALLEN LEAVES TO THEIR TREES

Autumn leaves are only really destined for one thing: kicking. Learning doesn't really cut it when you can be hurling, whirling and flinging up a wild storm of orange, red and brown. But sometimes, when you've kicked yourself into a stupor and you need some time to regroup before the next battle, a quieter activity has its (brief) merits. That's where this one comes in. Try to match the leaves around you to their trees. The illustrations opposite will help you to learn common leaf shapes and recognise tree outlines.

Alder

Ash

Beech

Silver
Birch

Hawthorn

Field
Maple

Sessile
Oak

Rowan

Sycamore

Crack
Willow

Horse
Chestnut

Alder

Ash

Beech

Silver
Birch

Hawthorn

Field
Maple

Sessile
Oak

Rowan

Sycamore

Crack
Willow

Horse
Chestnut

DO SOME LEAF RUBBINGS

This is a bit like wizardry. It's also magically money saving if you use it for DIY greetings cards.

1 Go out and collect leaves.

2 Place them on a flat surface and arrange them into a good pattern.

3 Lay a sheet of thinish paper over the top.

4 Hold a crayon lengthways and, pressing down, roll it along the paper so that the veins of the leaves are imprinted on the paper.

Toddlers should just go wild.

Older children should think about pattern and colours. If they are very careful, they can make stripy leaves, using several colours on each leaf.

MAKE AN AUTUMN LEAF GARLAND

These make good party decorations for Halloween, Bonfire Night or, if you're into that sort of thing, Mabon – a pagan ritual celebrated at the autumn equinox around 21 September. It marks the point at which the harvest is winding down, the fields are empty and the crops have been stored away. The idea is to take a moment to give thanks for these, as well as any other blessings that will carry us through winter. Which sounds quite nice, really, even if robes and beards aren't one of your top looks.

1 Collect some leaves, in lots of different shapes and colours.

2 Thread a long length of cotton onto a needle and push it through the stems of your leaves.

3 Arrange the leaves along the length of the thread.

Note Try painting patterns onto your leaves too, or tracing their veins in bright colours.

MAKE SNAP CARDS

If your kid is going through an extended competitive phase, these might be just your thing.

1 Collect leaves. You need two of each shape.

2 Cut squares from card, or thin cardboard like empty cereal packets, just big enough to fit your leaves onto.

3 Water down some PVA glue a little, and coat your squares in it.

4 Stick a leaf on each.

5 Brush the PVA-glue solution over the top of each.

6 Leave to dry.

7 Now play snap!

MAKE AN AUTUMN WREATH

Yes, yes, you can make a far more sophisticated wreath if you want to wrestle with wire and glue guns, buy in some mysterious material called 'burlap', and spend hours muttering and stabbing your fingers while the children tiptoe to the telly. Or you could do this.

1 Cut out the middle of a paper plate to leave a simple 'wreath' shape (a giant polo mint, basically).

2 Collect autumn leaves. Find as many as you can in lots of bright colours.

3 Give your cardboard wreath a decent coat of PVA glue.

4 Now stick your leaves onto the cardboard, making sure you cover every inch and have leaves sticking out at jolly angles. You might need extra blobs of glue so use it liberally.

5 Leave to dry before hanging your wonky, imperfect wreath proudly on the front door.

Older children can make this look really quite beautiful. They could try making patterns or dividing the wreath into different sections by leaf shape or colour. They can even make an 'ombre' effect by arranging the colours so that they fade from red to brown across the wreath.

BUILD A BUTTERFLY

Specifically, a Brimstone butterfly. Male Brimstones are bright yellow, like butter. They come out in spring but autumn leaves are perfect for recreating the veined, leaf-like appearance of the wings.

1 Look for fallen leaves – the more yellow, the better.

2 Draw the shape of a butterfly on paper.

3 Add your leaves to the wings you've drawn, dotting each with glue to stick it down and overlapping the leaves like butterfly scales.

4 Add a strip of wood bark (or a twig) for your butterfly's body. Pine needles are ideal for the antennae.

GO ON AN EVERGREEN HUNT

Which trees are still green? How many can you find?

MAKE A HALLOWEEN MASK

You could be a sprite, a lion, an owl… whatever you like. Making this mask is a) cheaper and less stressful than the usual last-minute dash to a shop, and b) guarantees you won't bump into anyone with the same costume – the ultimate trick-or-treating faux pas.

1 Draw the outline of the mask on a paper plate. If you're aiming for a 'sprite' it might just be two slim ovals. If you want a 'lion', then a circle with round ears protruding from the top and a shaggy mane all around it will be what you need. If an 'owl' is your favoured look you might want to make two fat circles, merged in the middle, with a couple of shaggy eyebrows poking out of their tops and a little beak between their bases.

2 Find lots of colourful leaves and practise arranging them on your mask. A lion's 'bushy' mane will require big orange leaves, and its face might be covered in smaller yellow ones. An owl will need rings of short, darker leaves around the eyes, paler leaves elsewhere and two long, 'bushy' leaves for 'eyebrows'. For a sprite, well, just go wild.

3 Glue the leaves into place and leave to dry.

4 Use a pencil to pierce a hole in each side of the mask, then cut two pieces of string and tie one end of each through a hole.

5 Tie the strings behind your head, and head out to pillage the neighbourhood of its stock of sweets.

MAKE A HURRICANE

1 Find a really big leaf pile and sort through it, quickly, to get rid of any hard objects like stones or bits of wood (or animal poo!).

2 Ermmm… hurl the leaves around. REALLY FAST!

HEDGEROWS

We must have had delayed onset heatstroke from the summer sun – or temporary insanity caused by withdrawal from the holidays. Either way, one day in early autumn we somehow found ourselves clawing our way up a hillside – with a child on each of our backs plus two tons of superfluous camping paraphernalia – on our way to an experimental eco-community living completely off grid somewhere in the nearby forest.

Tinkers Bubble, the community in question, was home to around 20 people at the time of writing, ranging from children to the elderly, who all live and work permanently on the land, making their hobbit-like homes from natural and recycled materials and their livings without the use of fossil fuels. We were to stay there for a mere week.

For seven days, from sunrise to sunset, we were outdoors. We ate in the open air, played in the open air, napped in the open air and threw open-air tantrums. But most of all, we worked, hard, in the open air.

We scythed, dug, forked, heaved and sawed for our suppers, the kids trailing behind. Johnny helped, kicked fallen fruit, climbed trees and complained in equal measure. Frida played in a wheelbarrow or crawled after rolling apples. Jim the carthorse ploughed the potato field while we all ran along behind him, shaking the treasure he unearthed into buckets. When we wanted to wash, we chopped wood, stoked the stove in the communal bath hut and... waited for three hours for it to warm the water.

Gradually, we got into the groove. We rammed down food, our bodies ravenously hungry for each meal, for the first time in years. We forgot about phones, computers and other stuff with screens. Our sleep was sounder, our minds clearer, our lungs cleaner and our bodies absolutely filthy.

The kids joined a tribe of tiny troglodytes who skipped, clambered, ran and rolled fearlessly over tree roots and up hillsides with the balance and agility of Olympians. TV was turfed out by farm jobs, a few wooden toys and the surrounding trees – forgotten, entirely, amid the all-consuming business of work and adventure. But best of all, since it was the start of autumn, was the almost unseemly, glutinous hoard of hedgerow fruits. Blackberries bleeding over small mouths and clothes, or smeared onto paper and the bark of trees. Apples for eating, catching and kicking. Sloes for squashing, squeezing and smearing under fingers and feet.

It was amazing. Life changing. Inspiring. And boy did those fingers and toes need scrubbing when we got home.

- The Romans used elderberry juice as hair dye.
- Hawthorn has a brilliant array of folk names, including azzies, aglets, asogs, arzy-garzies, boojuns and hoppety-haws.
- A huge number of Britain's hedgerows have been there for over a thousand years. Some mark medieval boundaries.
- Since the Second World War, some hedgerows have been obliterated to make way for buildings and bigger fields. There are now about 450,000 km (28,000 miles) of hedgerow left.
- Mice, voles and hedgehogs nest and feed in hedgerows, while bats use them as 'commuter routes' for foraging and birds nest in them.
- Hedgerows are great for the planet, storing carbon, capturing pollutants and helping to prevent soil erosion.

TOOLKIT TO TAKE

Jam jar
Paper
Brushes
Salt
Cotton cloth
Knife
Paint
Takeaway containers
Pencil
White cloth/t-shirt
String
Scissors

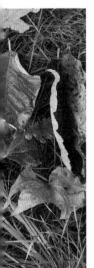

EAT NOW

Brambles (blackberries)

Cultivated apple

Wild strawberry

Crab apple

Hawthorn

EAT LATER

Elderberries

Sloe or Blackthorn

Damson

Rosehips

IDEAS TO START WITH

PICK AND MIX

We usually have good intentions when we go out picking. We scour scrubland, canal paths and wooded areas – looking for berries and other fruits for fun projects. But somehow, no matter how many we pick, we only ever finish up with a very thin layer at the bottom of the bucket. I have no idea how this happens.

1 Go out, with a hungry stomach and empty pockets, to hunt for fruit. You need wild spots, where brambles and hedgerows are free to spread, but they can be small ones. We've found fruits on the edges of abandoned lots, and even around the back of our local train station.

2 Keep one pocket, bucket or takeaway container for 'things to eat now' – the fruits that can be devoured on the spot, after a quick rinse.

3 Keep the other for 'keep and cook' – the fruits that need to be tarted up (or jammed up, chutneyed up and so on) in the kitchen before consumption.

Eat now...
Brambles (blackberries)
Apples
Wild strawberries

Eat later...
Crab apples
Sloes
Elderberries
Damsons
Rosehips
Hawthorn

MAKE NATURAL PAINTS

This is so good and messy that kids can, sometimes, be persuaded to leave some of their blackberries uneaten for the purpose.

1 Collect a selection of berries. Look for berries of different colours. You'll need a couple of decent handfuls of each.

2 When you're done, put the different berries in different containers (jam jars and takeaway boxes will do nicely), and mash them into a pulp with your hands or a stick.

3 Add water to make a paste.

4 Dip a brush into each pot and paint with the paste. See what different colours the berries make.

Older children can experiment with textures. They can try making a fine pulp to produce a realistic paint. Or mixing the berries, to see if they can create subtler shades. They can also have a think about things they can paint in these colours. We've found sunsets are good.

Note Do remember that some berries are poisonous. So wash hands and make sure you don't lick them!

GO APPLE BOBBING (WITHOUT GETTING WET)

1 Forage for apples that have a decent stalk attached.

2 Cut some long lengths of string.

3 Tie one end of the string tightly around the stalk of an apple.

4 Loop the other end around a tree's branch, adjusting the length so the apples hang at head height for the children involved.

5 Repeat until you've hung all your apples, then you're ready to hold the competition...

6 Contestants each line up in front of their apple, arms held behind their backs.

7 On the command 'Go!' each child has to try to grab their apple in their mouth, without using their hands.

MAKE NATURAL MAKE-UP

If you've pounded up only berries that are edible (and are sure of that), try using the pulp as make-up. Dab a little of the mixture onto your cheek and spread it around to make a blusher. Do the same on your lips to tint them. Remember, if you're going wild, it can be hard to scrub off.

...OR BLOOD

If your mood's more murderous than make-up (or if it's Halloween), try daubing yourself in pulped edible berries and making it look as convincingly as possible like blood. Dribble the pulp from the corner of your mouth, or if it's still quite thick, try giving yourself a dripping gunshot to the temple.

DO SOME APPLE PRINTING

Just as fun as potato printing, this.

1   Go outside and find some windfall apples, or damaged bought ones if you can't find any on the ground.

2   Cut the apples in half (if you slice straight down from the stem, you'll get a blank canvas to work with; if you slice the other way, you'll reveal a ready-made star shape to print with, made from the holes that the pips hide in).

3   Draw a simple shape onto the flat surface.

4   Now use your knife to very carefully score around the outside of the shape and cut away the surrounding apple.

5   Brush paint onto your shape, then gently press it onto a piece of paper.

6   Lift the apple and see the shape left in paint.

Toddlers will need some help to do the cutting but younger children can do the prints themselves.

Older children This is a good way for them to make DIY wrapping paper.

LEARN TO JUGGLE WITH APPLES

Because everybody needs a party trick...

1   Find two apples on the ground.

2   Hold one in each hand.

3   Throw one apple up and over to the opposite hand.

4   Just before you catch it, throw the second apple over to the empty hand.

5   Catch the first apple and keep going...

Older children Add more apples as soon as they get cocky.

TRY FOOT TREADING

In the Douro region of Portugal, famed for its production of port, grapes are harvested, transported into *lagares* – large, shallow tanks – then stomped all over, unceremoniously, by a bare-footed team of workers. It's believed to be the optimum method of breaking up the grapes and kneading their skins to extract the colour and flavour for port. It's also a lot of fun. Our *lagare* is usually a takeaway container, and our 'grapes' are berries, but the method is exactly the same and, just like in Portugal, you won't want to drink the results unless your feet are extremely clean.*

1   Collect as many non-poisonous berries as you can fit into two takeaway containers.

2   Take off your shoes and socks and roll up your trousers. If you want to try drinking the juice, wash your feet thoroughly.

3   Put one foot in each container and stomp wildly all over the berries, squeezing them between your toes until you have a satisfying pulp.

*Even if you don't drink the result, it's still quite fun to pound the berries.

MAKE NATURAL DYES

Would you call these last two suggestions cheating? I hope not. You do need a few additions to the toolkit to do this and the following activity, but nothing you wouldn't find in your kitchen so it shouldn't cost you a bean. Or a berry…

1 Find a 'white something' to dye. You can use old pieces of cotton from your toolkit or, if you'd rather, an old white T-shirt that needs a facelift.

2 In your kitchen, before you go out, add half a cup of salt to eight cups of cold water in a pan, plop in your fabric and simmer for an hour.

3 Now go out and hunt for blackberries. You want at least enough to fill your takeaway container. If you can't find blackberries, elderberries or other dark edible berries will do.

4 Mash or chop your berries into a pulp.

5 Now put them in a pan with twice as much plain water.

6 Bring the water to the boil, then let it simmer for 45 minutes.

7 Now strain the water to get rid of the 'bits'.

8 Take out the fabric from the salt water, rinse it, give it a squeeze, then add it to the hot, strained dye and simmer for an hour.

9 Turn off the heat and leave the fabric to soak. Overnight is best.

10 In the morning take out the fabric, squeeze it out, then hang it up to dry

11 When dry, it'll be naturally purple!

Older children If they have some elastic bands, they can make tie-dye. They can grab a handful of the material and tie it tightly with an elastic band, then repeat a few times in different places before putting the fabric into the dye. They should untie the bands when they take out the fabric, then see what patterns they've made.

MAKE A HEDGEROW JAM

The wonderful thing about it is that you can use any old edible hedgerow berries. And it's simple. Even for us.

1. Check your kitchen for the following simple ingredients: half a lemon, and 500 g (1.1 lb) sugar. That's it.

2. Go outside and pick as many edible hedgerow berries and apples as you can find. You want roughly an equal weight of each.

3. Go home and weigh your finds. You want (roughly, again) 400 g (0.9 lb) of berries and 400 g of apples (0.9 lb) but you can adjust the amounts according to what you've harvested...

4. Chop your apples and put them in a pan with your berries, the juice of half a lemon and 60 ml (2 fl oz) of water.

5. Simmer gently over a low heat till it's all soft and pulpy.

6. Add the sugar and stir till it's dissolved.

7. Turn the heat up and boil rapidly till it reaches setting point (careful here, it's extremely hot).

8. To test the setting point, use a teaspoon to drop a blob of the jam on a chilled saucer. Leave it for a minute then poke it. If it wrinkles, it is set.

9. Leave it to cool, then spoon into a clean jar. Sterilise the jar first by putting it in the dishwasher or in a warm oven for a while, filling it while it's still hot.

MUD

Mud – as far as the eye could see. Mud shovelled to the edges of the runway as we touched down in Stockholm airport. Mud splashed up the sides of the taxi into which we fell, windscreen wipers whirling as it sped through a pitch-black, fairytale nightscape. Mud on the queue of waterproof trousers lined up at the bus station the following morning. And now here we were, up to our ankles in it, Johnny and I, encircled by Goretex-garmented children, holding hands like little muddy Michelin men, singing a song about a Swedish troll named Olle Bolle.

Thus were we welcomed to Forest School. The concept of schools and nurseries in which the vast majority of the day is spent outdoors has now spread across Sweden and to the rest of the world. We, though, had come to see the original, the first and arguably the best: *I Ur och Skur* ('rain or shine') in Lidingö, just north-east of Stockholm.

Siw Linde, who founded the school in 1985, explained that it is based on a philosophy that nature is not just the perfect playground but an ideal classroom, too, nurturing children's innate curiosity, companionability, cooperation, concentration, climbing and even conservation.

Roughly 80 per cent of their time is spent outdoors, though if the wind is really strong or the temperature drops below – 10º C (28º F) the children will go inside for a portion of the day.

They definitely don't let a little bit of mud get in their way, however. So off we stomped, up a forested hillside, a sea of waterproof suits in varying sizes: six-year-olds stopping to lift two-year-olds over difficult terrain, or pausing along the way to examine a mossy rock. At the top of the hill a simple tarpaulin was erected between some trees and... the children disappeared. Some I spotted wading in a shallow stream. Down a slope, a girl clambered to the top of a worryingly wobbly tree. Someone else was determinedly dragging a large sheet of corrugated iron through the mud. It looked like choas, except for the uncanny calm and the startling degree of collaboration between children in their various muddy endeavours.

'Don't they ever get hurt?' I asked Siw. She shrugged. 'I think a boy once broke his wrist a number of years ago,' she said. 'But he was actually under his father's supervision at the time. We never lift a child up into a tree, so they need to have mastered the climbing skills to get up there in the first place. They can, therefore, get down again. They know their capabilities.'

It's true, I realise. It may look scary, but it isn't. Given relative freedom, the kids don't kill themselves, each other or the environment. In fact, they seem to take more responsibility for all those things than the average anarchic primary schoolchild. Soon, they wander back and gather under the tarpaulin for a snack and a hot drink. They listen attentively to a teacher who tells a story with some small wooden dolls; they play memory and counting games with fallen leaves, pine cones and conkers; they sing some songs, play a game, and then it's time for us to leave them.

'What do you think British schools could learn from Forest Schools?' I asked Johnny on the bus home. 'More mud?' he said, thoughtfully. 'Oh, and warm juice.'

FACTS TO FIRE THE IMAGINATION

- Mud is an Old English word dating back to at least 1400.
- Muddy play might actually boost your mood due to microscopic bacteria called *Mycobacterium vaccae*, which increase the level of serotonin in our brains, helping us to relax.
- If you feed that *Mycobacterium vaccae* to mice, they can navigate their way through mazes twice as fast as usual.
- Ancient Egyptians used mud bricks to build their houses.
- Mud baths are taken to help alleviate pains and muscle aches. Their mineral-rich content is also thought to have a soothing effect.

TOOLKIT TO TAKE

Trowel
Jam jar
Foil takeaway containers
Yoghurt pots
Paper
Brushes
Tray or plastic bag

MAKE ADOBE (MUD) BRICKS

In my experience this can be done in one of two ways: 1) you've spent the last six days watching kids' shows on Netflix and therefore, stricken with guilt, dress it up as a 'learning' exercise in historic building practices, or 2) you either haven't or have given up caring and therefore declare it a 'Bob the Builder bonanza'. Both entirely and equally legitimate.

1   Go outside somewhere where you can pick up thick mud, grass, leaves and twigs.

2   Tear up your grass and leaves, and break your twigs into small pieces, keeping them in separate piles.

3   Find some good, sticky mud.

4   In one takeaway box or yoghurt pot, thoroughly mix the mud with the twigs, making sure it's a good, thick consistency – not sloppy.

5   Fill it to the top.

6   In the next box, use the same technique with the leaves. In another, use the grass.

7   Now leave your concoctions to set into bricks. They need to be somewhere warm for a day or two, so really you need to bring them inside and put them near the radiator (sorry, Mum). If you don't fancy waiting for days, stick them in the oven at a very low temperature for a few hours, till they are hard to the touch.

8   Once dry, try popping the bricks out of their moulds and testing which one is the strongest.

USE YOUR BRICKS TO BUILD A FAIRY HOUSE

1   Place two of your bricks side by side, leaving a gap between them.

2   Lay the last brick over the top, like a roof.

3   Now decorate your house with leaves and autumn foliage.

4   You can add a garden made from moss, leaves or grass, and even build a twig fence round it.

BE A BEAVER AND BUILD A MUD DAM

Beavers build dams from sticks and mud as protection from predators and to provide access to food. If a buck-toothed giant rodent can do it, you can too.

1   Beavers build their dams in shallow moving water, often in places where the flow is already constricted. So, ideally, find a place in a stream where there are some ready-made obstacles to work with (a tree stump, tight bend or rocks, for example). Otherwise you can practise on a puddle.

2   Beavers then use their teeth and front paws to move mud, stones, sticks and branches from the stream's bottom to the site of their dam. You can do likewise, (using your hands, not your teeth), or scavenge around the banks for materials. Beavers carry the larger sticks in their mouths (not advised for children).

3   Like beavers do, you can then build the dam from the bottom up, plastering together the natural materials with mud. Big things, like branches, go at the bottom to anchor the dam. Twigs, brush, plants and leaves go on top to build up the structure.

4   When finished, the top of the dam should be sticking up above the water

5   See how long it holds! When you're done, leave everything as you found it.

MAKE A MUD CASTLE

Build yours just like a sandcastle but with mud instead of sand. Shell decorations should also be replaced by stones, sticks and leaves and, importantly, ice-cream refreshments by hot chocolate.

BE A MUD SCULPTOR

It doesn't have to be a castle, remember. Get your hands involved and mould the mud into anything you fancy – maybe a mudman instead of a snowman? You are still entitled to hot chocolate.

COOK WITH MUD

Can you make a mud pie? Or a mud milkshake? Perhaps mud sausages? Use a stick for stirring stews, and hands for shaping pies and bangers. Water down your milkshake to the desired consistency in a jam jar. Use a takeaway box, too, for added authenticity.

TAKE OFF YOUR SHOES AND SOCKS AND… STOMP

Yep… sorry again, Mum and Dad, but wriggling your toes in mud is really a human right. Try other textures, too, like wet grass or leaf piles (but make sure there are no hidden nasties like litter about).

Note Get out a sheet of paper, while you're at it, and try making muddy hand and foot prints on it. Leave to dry and display with pride.

PAINT WITH MUD

In 1988 an artist called Richard Long dipped pages into wet mud taken from the River Avon in Bristol, hung them up to drip and dry, called them drawings and sold them to the Tate Gallery in London. Yeah, I'm not sure, either, but it's got to be worth a shot.

1   In a takeaway box, water down some mud and mix with a stick till you have a good brown paint.
2   Now either use a brush to paint the mud onto paper, or follow Long's lead and dip the paper straight into the mixture.

Note If you don't have paper, or fancy a change, you can try painting patterns onto fallen leaves or tree trunks with a brush.

MAKE WAR PAINT

Paper is all well and good, but sometimes the best canvas is your own face. Dip your fingers in mud and drag stripes across your face to give yourself some war paint.

MAKE A GREEN MAN'S FACE

Green Jack, Jack-in-the-Green and Green George – in legend, the green man goes by many names, but most agree he is a pagan god who roams the woodlands of Europe, wearing a pair of horns on his head and peering out of a mask of branches and leaves. Other than that, anything goes, so use your imagination. Just remember, he has rain-making powers. So don't make him cross.

1 Find some thick, sticky mud.

2 Choose a nearby tree trunk.

3 Stick the mud to the tree trunk, gradually moulding it into the shape of a face (if your mud isn't thick enough to stay in place, add torn-up grass and leaves to the mixture).

4 Now hunt for fallen foliage to make the features: moss might make a good beard, acorns or their caps are excellent eyes and ferns offer up good eyebrow material.

MAKE A MUD SLIDE

1 Find a muddy slope with open space at the bottom of it.

2 Sit at the top on a plastic bag or tray.

3 Ask a friend to give you a good shove on the count of three.

4 Slide down, as fast as you can!

5 Load the washing machine.

DECORATE YOUR WELLIES

Paint mud patterns onto them.

HUNT FOR ANIMAL PRINTS

See which of these you can find imprinted in the mud. Can you follow a trail of footprints to see where an animal has gone?

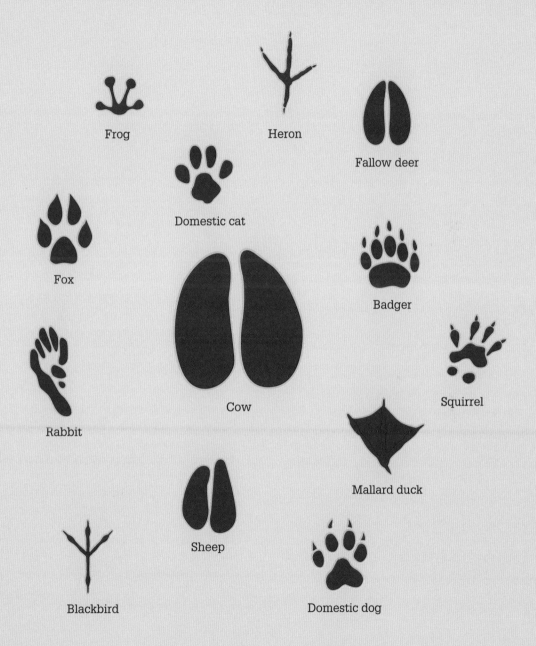

Frog

Heron

Fallow deer

Domestic cat

Fox

Badger

Cow

Squirrel

Rabbit

Mallard duck

Sheep

Blackbird

Domestic dog

MUSHROOMS AND MOSS

Think back in time, to almost 500 million years ago, further even than the time when, as my son likes to say, 'dinosaurs were around and Mummy was a little girl'.

The world was a very different place: the seas were teeming with life while the land was rocky and barren. But something was happening. The first, very early forms of plant life were moving from the water, onto the land. And among them, we think, were early forms of moss.

They might not have looked like much, but the arrival of these adventurous bryophytes (that's mosses, liverworts and hornworts) was one of the most important events in Earth's history. They changed global climates and soils, and helped all forms of multi-cellular terrestrial life to evolve and spread across the world.

Much of this process is still mysterious. For example, in 1859 an enigmatic fossil was unearthed of an organism that dates from between 420 and 370 million years ago. Large, trunk-like structures, reaching up to a whopping 8 m (26 ft) tall (imagine a mature oak tree), these organisms, known as Prototaxites, towered over any other life form of the period.

Debate over what they might be raged, and continues still. But in 2007 a study claimed that they were, in fact, a fungus – like a gigantic, early mushroom.

It seems possible that while mosses (and other bryophytes) had the land to themselves for a long while, mushrooms were also once its most imposing feature. And then came children...

Well okay, there were some other, minor, steps in between. Dinosaurs, sabre-toothed tigers and so on. But it was surely children who really shook things up. Out they charged from their homes, overturning the logs that had sheltered the mushrooms' dark, damp homes, stomping over moss, sniffing mushrooms and mashing moss with wellies. Things would never be the same again.

So as you venture into the woods, don't forget to stop and marvel at moss and mushrooms. They once ruled the world. Before kids became the bosses.

FACTS TO FIRE THE IMAGINATION

- The Giant Puffball mushroom can grow bigger than a person's head and contains up to 7 trillion spores.
- Ink made from the Shaggy Inkcap mushroom was used to sign the Magna Carta in 1215.
- The largest living organism ever discovered is a honey mushroom called *Armillaria ostoyae*. It covered some 10 km² (4 sq miles) in Oregon, USA – the equivalent of 1,665 football fields.
- There are around 12,000 species of moss in the world.
- During the First World War mosses were used as bandages.
- Some mosses are indicators of pollution. Because they are so good at absorbing nitrogen, if overloaded they quickly deteriorate.

TOOLKIT TO TAKE

PVA glue
Brush
Paper
Jam jar
Paints
Knife
Card
Magnifying glass

Always remember to all wash your hands extremely thoroughly after touching mushrooms.

GO ON A MUSHROOM SCAVENGER HUNT

You may have a child who understands the instruction '*Don't* touch'. I've heard they do exist, somewhere. If not, do ensure, at least, that they don't eat any mushrooms, and wash their hands when you're done hunting.

How many different kinds can you find? How many different sizes, shapes and colours do they come in? Search in:

- Damp places.
- Places with lots of rotting tree matter.
- Around the bases of trees.
- In leaf piles.
- In mossy areas.

MAKE MUSHROOM INK

Good and mucky, this...

1. Go out and find some Shaggy Inkcap mushrooms. They're easy to identify and are not poisonous, so are totally safe to muck around with. Look on grass, roadsides and rubbish heaps for big mushrooms with a ring around their stem, an outside that's white and looks like it has scales and an inside that's black.

2. Pick off the tops from the mushrooms and stick them in a jam jar.

3. Now leave them for a few days, ideally outside as this stage can be smelly. Slowly, your mushrooms will liquefy into a dark ink.

4. When ready, dip a brush into the jam jar and use the ink to paint on paper.

Note Always wash your hands after touching mushrooms. If you're unsure what kind they are don't pick them and don't eat them.

DISSECT A MUSHROOM

One for the forensic scientists…

1 Go out and find some mushrooms, and pick them carefully. Make sure you leave plenty for nature

2 Wash your hands.

3 Take a magnifying glass and examine a mushroom closely. Can you find the parts shown below?

4 Use a knife to separate the mushroom into its parts and examine them more closely. What textures and colours can you find?

5 Wash your hands again, for good measure.

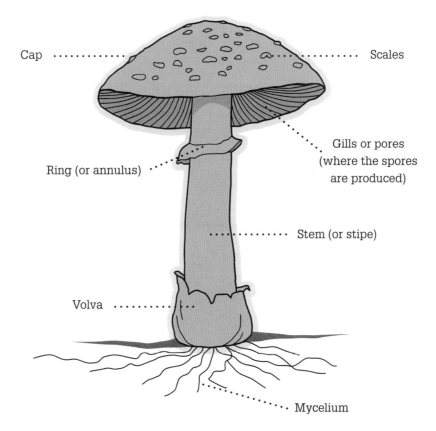

Cap

Scales

Gills or pores
(where the spores
are produced)

Ring (or annulus)

Stem (or stipe)

Volva

Mycelium

FIND A FAIRY RING AND STEP INSIDE

In German folklore fairy rings are said to mark the spot where witches have danced. In Holland they were believed to be the places where the Devil rested his milk churn. In France fairy rings are guarded by giant, bug-eyed toads. Wherever you happen to be when you find a naturally occurring circle of mushrooms growing, you have to be extremely brave to step inside it.

BUILD A FAIRY DEN

Traditionally, fairies lived in and around the white spotted, red-capped *Amanita muscaria* mushroom. But times are changing. House prices are rocketing, mortgages are hard to come by and housing stock is in short supply. They can't afford to be so picky these days. Here's how to give them a hand by creating your own 'affordable housing' scheme.

1   Find a tall, solid-looking mushroom with a good, wide cap under which a fairy could shelter.
2   Look for furniture. An acorn cap makes a good basin, bowl or even loo. A pile of shredded grass is an excellent bed, and the hollow interior of a conker case makes a fine bath.
3   Arrange your furniture under the mushroom and leave it for a lucky house-hunting fairy to find.

MAKE A SPORE PRINT

Make a print without paint or ink. It's a natural magic trick.

1   Pick a toadstool and carefully break off the stem (if you have any going spare at home, you can do this with shop-bought mushrooms too).
2   Put the cap on a piece of pale card, the right way up (with its underside on the paper).
3   Cover with a jam jar and leave overnight.
4   In the morning you'll find that the spores have landed on your card and left a pattern.

Older children Explain that this works because each mushroom produces millions of microscopic spores – seed-like cells that grow into mushrooms themselves.

Note Different fungi leave different spore prints, so why not try a few?

MAKE A JAM-JAR TERRARIUM

... which is really just a posh way of saying 'miniature ecosystem'. It's like an aquarium, but for plants instead of fish – a small world in a glass jar. Who doesn't want one of those?

1   Find a handful of pebbles and put them into a jam jar to create the base-layer of your 'terrarium'.

2   Sprinkle some soil on top to create a thickish layer, then wet it lightly with water.

3   Now find some moss. Look in the cracks in pavements and garden walls, and on trees and rocks. Use a knife to carefully prise off the moss.

4   Drop the sections of moss into the jar, green side up, so that you have a mossy layer on top.

5   Water the moss lightly every day, and cross your fingers in the hope that it will grow! Watch through the glass to see white roots pushing down through the soil.

6   Optional: put some small plastic animals (that includes dinosaurs) on top, so that they can roam about on the moss.

Note If you want to do this really professionally and keep your terrarium for longer, you can put a layer of charcoal between the pebbles and soil. It'll help filter the water so your terrarium will stay fragrant.

MAKE A MOSS COLLAGE

It turns out, once you unleash your imagination, that moss is oddly versatile stuff. We have cut and collaged it into anything from lush hillsides, green dinosaurs, luminous snot and alien eyebrows. Arrange it on the ground, using twigs, stones and leaves to make the rest of your picture, or use a brush and glue to stick it onto paper, painting on the rest of the image – it's up to you.

TAKE THE MOSS, MUSHROOM AND LICHEN CHALLENGE

There are more than 10,000 species of moss in the world. Set your family a challenge to find them. Don't stop until you've seen all of them. Or it's time for supper. Don't be a quitter, now...

MAKE YOURSELF A MOSS-TACHE

You'll be amazed how hilarious you all look with a strip of moss balanced on your top lips...

WIND

I've tried to think of ways to sugar-coat the truth. Because wind is, of course, an incredible thing.

It's caused by the gases of the Earth's atmosphere moving about in an attempt to equalise pressure, and when you think of it like that, it's a pretty awesome phenomenon. It's fantastic if you are a seasick sailor, yearning for home. Or a hipster with a windmill, a hefty mortgage and dreams about the boutique/organic/heritage grain flour vogue. Or, a renewable energy entrepreneur in a hard hat, surveying her field of wind turbines. Or a migrating bird with the avian equivalent of tennis elbow, hoping to catch a free ride and some respite for his wings. Or even a windsurfer, a paraglider or some other breed of thrill seeker with a death wish.

For the rest of us, though, in general, it sucks. If you are very small it knocks you flat, so that one minute you are bending to inspect a worm and the next you find yourself face down and bewildered in a pile of yellow leaves. If you are marginally larger it pushes and pulls at you like the playground bully and spills the hot chocolate you've poured in an attempt to be brave about the weather and warm up. If you are huge ('like Mum or an elephant', as the kids would add as a helpful point of reference), it makes your eyes sting, plays havoc with your hair and brings you out in inelegant red blotches.

We've tried, we really have. But, while we're aware that our failure to embrace it might leave us relegated to the ranks of (quite literally) fair-weather naturalists, we are not wild about wind. Still, sometimes the alternative is worse. When, for example, your entire family has turned practically translucent through lack of contact with natural light. Or when the walls of the house are shaking because of the people bouncing off them. On such occasions you have to fill a Thermos with whatever you find

most strengthening, and try to make a virtue of necessity. Use your opponent's strength against him, as Bruce Lee would say. Make wind part of the game. (Why can I hear my family sniggering?)

FACTS TO FIRE THE IMAGINATION

- The fastest wind speed not related to tornadoes ever recorded was on 10 April 1996, when a weather station on Barrow Island, Australia, registered a maximum wind gust of 408 km/h (253 mph).
- You get wind in outer space, too. Solar winds are streams of charged particles that escape the Sun's gravity.
- Neptune is the windiest planet in the solar system.
- People in China were using windmills to pump water and grind grain in as early as 200BC.
- Today, the world's largest wind turbine is in Hawaii and is 20 storeys tall. Its blades alone are as long as football fields.

TOOLKIT TO TAKE

PVA glue
Brush
Paper
Scissors
Sellotape
Jam jar
Needle and thread
Paints
String
Pencil
Plastic straw
Plastic bag
Marker pen

IDEAS TO START WITH

HOLD A HELICOPTER-SEED COMPETITION

An old favourite, this. The Sycamore is so hardy that it can grow in places that would thwart other trees. Maybe that's why you can find the trees in almost every park in our city (just don't expect your helicopters to travel spectacular distances).

1 Go for a walk with a friend and collect helicopter seeds in different shapes and sizes.

2 Mark your collection so that you can tell which seeds are yours and which belong to your friend (blobs of paint in a different colour from those of your friend will do nicely, or different shapes drawn in marker pen).

3 Now find a high place to stand on: it could be a hill, the top of a slide or even a low wall.

4 See which way the wind is blowing (lick a finger and hold it above your head, then rotate it until you feel the wind's chill hitting the pad of your finger).

5 Take turns to launch your helicopter seeds in the direction that the wind is moving, and watch them spin off into the distance.

6 When you're done, climb down and find your collection. The winner is the person with the helicopter seed that has travelled furthest.

MAKE HELICOPTER-SEED DRAGONFLIES

1 Scavenge for the following: helicopter seeds with two wings intact and short twigs to make your dragonflies' bodies.

2 Paint the helicopter seeds with whatever pattern you fancy. You can paint the twig too if you want.

3 Leave to dry.

4 Cut long lengths of thread and snap your twigs to the right length for a dragonfly's body.

5 Dragonflies have two pairs of wings, one in front of the other, so position your helicopter-seed 'wings' over your twig 'body', then secure the back ones by winding the thread around them and knotting firmly.

6 Tie on the front pair of wings in the same fashion.

7 Attach another piece of string to the middle of the dragonfly and make a loop at the top so you can hang it from a branch to 'fly' in the wind.

Toddlers The tying is fiddly so they will need help. They will, however, be excellent at the painting stages.

STAGE A FLYING COMPETITION

I'm happy to admit that this activity was born out of desperation one disagreeably blustery day, mid-walk and mid-tantrum. It works, though. And it's easy. And it stopped the screaming and the flailing of limbs.

1 Forage for light objects: feathers, leaves, helicopter seeds (things that wouldn't hurt if they smacked you in the face, basically).

2 Take bets on which object will travel furthest in the wind.

3 One by one, hold each object above your head, wait for a gust of wind, shout '1,2,3 LIFT OFF!' then let it go, seeing how far the object is carried by the wind before falling to the ground.

MAKE A HELICOPTER-SEED BUMBLEBEE

Same same, but different...

1 Find some small pine cones for your bumblebee's body, as well as some helicopter seeds with just one wing attached.

2 Paint a pine cone (if you want) in yellow and black stripes and leave to dry.

3 Gently push two helicopter seeds into each side of the pine cone (seed in first) until the seeds are held firmly between the scales. Your bumblebee now has the requisite four wings!

4 Cut a length of string and wind one end around the middle of your pine cone, sliding it between scales as you go so that it becomes invisible, then tie it at the top.

5 Make a loop at the other end, and hang the bumblebee from a branch.

MAKE A MIGRATING SWALLOW

In late autumn many swallows undertake a pretty extraordinary adventure. Those that have summered in Britain, for instance, fly first across western France, then over the Pyrenees and down eastern Spain into Morocco, before finally crossing the Sahara to South Africa. They cover 320 km (200 miles) a day, at a maximum speed of 56 km (35 miles) per hour, sometimes in enormous flocks numbering hundreds of thousands of birds. I once drove 240 km (150 miles) to France with just my own family of four and the experience was near fatal, so you really have to hand it to the birds.

1 Photocopy the page opposite, or trace around it and then copy it onto a new piece of paper.

2 Fold your paper inwards along the centre line **A**.

3 Fold out each half along the diagonal lines **B**, so they meet together, then fold in along lines **C** and then lines **D**.

4 Use a small amount of Sellotape to stick down the flaps underneath and to hold lines **B** together to make the swallow on the top.

5 See how far you can make your swallow fly!

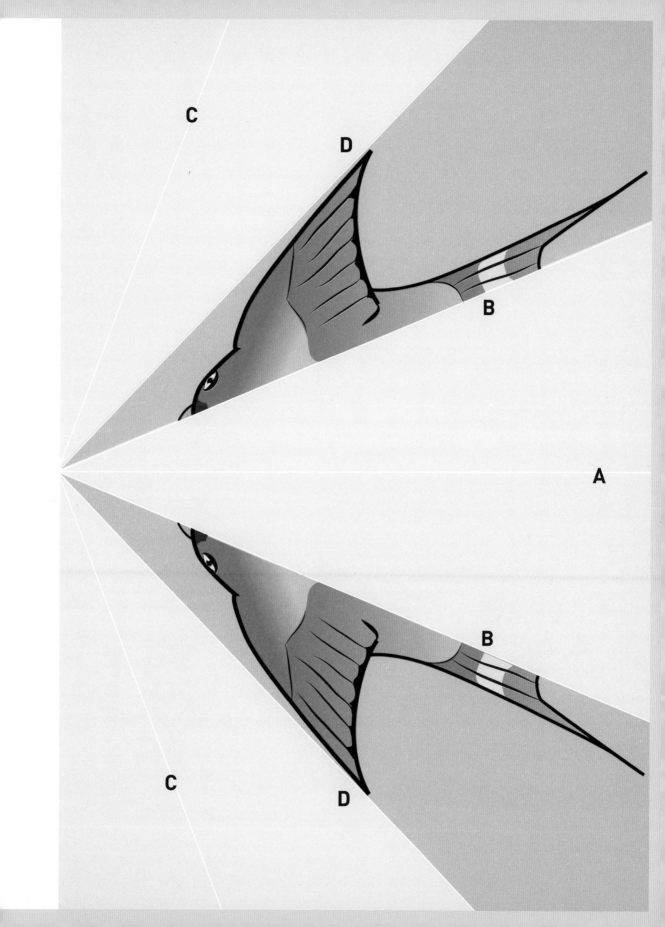

MAKE A WEATHER VANE

One for the mini meteorologists…

1   Find a bit of exposed ground on which to set up your weather vane.

2   Take a plastic straw. This is going to be the arm of your weather vane. Use scissors to make a snip in each end, about 1 cm (½ in) long (if you have a straw with a bendy bit at the top, cut that off first).

3   Use scissors to cut a small triangle and square of paper (each about 5 cm/2 in long).

4   Slip the triangle into one slit end of the straw, pointing outwards. Secure with Sellotape. Then add the square to the other end, securing it in the same way.

5   Find a very straight stick and drive one end into the soil, patting down the earth around it so that it stands perfectly and securely upright.

6   Now hold your straw so that the triangle and square are pointing up vertically (not lying flat). Drive a needle through the centre of the straw, from top to bottom.

7   Push the sharp end of the needle into the top of your stick, so that the straw sits on top of it, secured by the needle.

8   Blow on the paper square and see if the straw spins. If not, take the needle and reposition it ever so slightly in the straw.

9   Once the straw is evenly balanced, it will catch the wind and show you which direction it is blowing in.

Toddlers will need lots of help with this, especially the needle bit. But it's a good exercise for exploring the concept of wind.

TRY THE WINDMILL 'YOGA' POSE

1   Stand with your feet a little wider than shoulder-width apart and facing forwards. Breathe deeply.

2   Raise your arms to either side at shoulder height.

3   Bend forwards at the waist.

4   Reach down with your right hand to touch your left foot, and let your left hand point upwards towards the ceiling.

5   Hold this position for a couple of deep breaths, then...

6   Switch sides, raising your right hand back up towards the ceiling and lowering your left hand down to touch your right foot.

7   Wait for a couple of deep breaths, then swap over again. Repeat a few times.

I SPY...

Something that's fallen from up high. Head outside and challenge the kids to find ten things that have fallen to the ground in the wind (leaves, seeds and feathers, for example). The winner is the first to bring their ten finds back to base.

MAKE A SUPER-SIMPLE KITE

Once a week the kids now go to Forest School. Crouched under the trees, mixing mud pies, building dens and clambering over fallen trees, it's one of the highlights of our week. Here's one of their favourite activities.

1   Use one end of some string to tie together the handles of a plastic bag.
2   Unwind a decent length of the string, then run, letting the plastic bag trail behind you until it catches the wind, inflates and rises up into the air like a kite.

Okay, so Mary Poppins it ain't, but the thrill is just as electric.

USE THE BEAUFORT SCALE

In 1806 a British naval commander called Sir Francis Beaufort created a historic scale, still used today in Met Office marine forecasts for measuring wind intensity. It's brilliant for sailors and for us, too, since it requires no tools at all. Plus, it was later developed to include land measurements, so you don't even have to go to sea to be a great maritime hero yourself. All you have to do is take a stomp around your neighbourhood with this chart, looking out for the following things and what they are doing, then seeing where they are on the Beaufort scale.

- A chimney with smoke rising from it.
- A weather vane.
- A flag (presumably a more common sight in 19th-century neighbourhoods than in modern ones – don't get too hung up over finding one in yours).
- Paper litter on the ground.
- Leaves, small twigs and branches.
- Small trees.
- Tall trees.

THE BEAUFORT SCALE

Beaufort number 1
Light air movement, 1-3mph
Smoke drifts in direction of air,
vanes don't move

Beaufort number 2
Light breeze, 4-7mph
Wind felt on face, leaves rustle,
vanes begin to move, flags stir

Beaufort number 3
Gentle breeze, 8-12mph
Leaves and twigs move, light
flags start to extend

Beaufort number 4
Moderate breeze, 13-18mph
Dust, leaves and light paper rise
up, branches move, flags flap

Beaufort number 5
Fresh breeze, 19-24mph
Small trees begin to sway,
flags ripple

Beaufort number 6
Strong breeze, 25-31mph
Large branches move, flags
beat, whistling heard on wires

Beaufort number 7
Moderate gale, 32-38mph
Whole trees move, flags extend,
resistance is felt walking
into the wind

Beaufort number 8
Fresh gale, 39-46mph
Twigs and small branches
break off trees, walking
is difficult

Beaufort number 9
Strong gale, 47-54mph
Slate blown from roofs, some
structural damage

Beaufort number 10
Whole gale, 55-63mph
Seldom experienced on land,
trees broken, considerable
structural damage

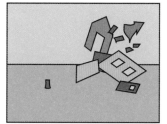

Beaufort number 11
Storm, 64-72mph
Very rarely experienced on land,
trees uprooted, major
structural damage

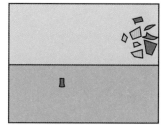

Beaufort number 12
Hurricane, 73mph or higher
Widespread devastation

WINTER

'All the leaves are gone, and the sky is grey! We're going for a walk! On a winter's daaaaaaaaay...' The words might be a little wrong but, as we stomp along, we are our own rock group – The Mamas and the Papas and the Daughters and the Sons and a gaggle of their Friends...

Right now, the 'Mamas' section of that equation is definitely dreaming of California. Because of course, when we say 'a walk', we don't mean it in the sense that any sane adult would understand. In our household, if a winter walk of more than a few dozen metres is to be undertaken with any degree of success, it either has to be a pilgrimage towards something sugary (then punctuated, every 60 seconds, by a reminder of that sugary mecca: 'REMEMBER THE CHOCOLATE/CAKE/CHOCOLATE-BISCUIT-CAKE!!!!'), or peppered with wild song and elaborate stories of dangerous adventure, interposed with pantomime gestures and regular diversions along walls or down lamp-posts.

Our postman is a little twitchy around us. Which is perfectly fair. We must look a little crazed. But the truth is quite the opposite. These outdoor excursions are what keep us sane.

Inside our house – through the radio, TV, Twitter and so on – news seems to reach us daily of the dangers that cooped-up lifestyles pose to children's bodies and minds. UNICEF, finding in 2011 that British children were amongst the least happy in the world, blamed parents for trapping their children in a cycle of 'compulsive consumerism' by showering them with classes, toys and designer labels instead of the thing they really crave: 'spending time with the people they love, being outdoors and doing fun activities'.

I know it's fashionable to blame the parents, but it doesn't seem quite fair. Back in 2010 the RSPB commissioned new research into childhood experiences of nature. It compiled a list of 12 outdoor experiences, like climbing trees, looking for insects and feeding birds, then it asked British adults how many they remembered experiencing in their own childhoods.

Every single one of the 12 activities was remembered by at least half of the people surveyed. The most evocative memories were of climbing trees and collecting or playing conkers, both of which were remembered by 70 per cent of the public surveyed. And, perhaps most significantly, a huge 92 per cent agreed it was important that children should experience those types of activities and encounters today.

I know that the magic of my own childhood was located in the long periods of 'nothing to do' it entailed. And of course, by nothing, I mean a lot. Because – as we ourselves discovered – if you stick some children outside, with nothing more structured than some snowballs at their disposal, a *lot* happens inside their heads.

There is something about the endless possibilities of some frozen water, a carrot and a handful of pebbles that cannot be replicated in plastic and technology, or even through the very best organised activities. Something that challenges and stretches the mind. And as Gever Tulley, founder of Tinkering School said in a TED Talk, 'We don't need another generation of kids who are really good at taking tests. What we need is generations of kids who see the really tough problems of the world as puzzles, and have the tenacity, the creative resources and the creative ability to solve those puzzles.'

But it's not always that simple and, despite our best intentions, by the end of the year everyone in our house seems to be a bit, well, frazzled. Homework, work-work, colds, chauffeuring, Christmas parties, cake, too much plonk and parental guilt – it all, seemingly unavoidably, leads to less and less time to spend just doing 'nothing' outside, and more and more time spent stressed out in front of screens.

It's a vicious circle in which, left unchecked, our bodies would grow ever rounder and our eyes ever squarer. You don't need to be a geometry genius to guess that this equation can never be balanced. So before our minds implode under the strain, here's a simple idea: how about, just occasionally, giving everyone, including the over-stretched, over-stressed, just-trying-to-do-the-right-thing-and-stay-awake-on-five-hours-sleep parent, a break?

It's in search of that break that our family goes outside. Let the fizzle of electricity dissipate in the puffs of cold air we breathe out. See our reflections in puddles instead of our screens. Stomp and stretch the legs that have been curled in front of TVs and under laptops. Let our boots do the work and give our brains the chance to wander, unleashed, unhindered and unhassled through the skies in the slipstreams of birds. And then we have hot chocolate.

- Globally, the number of overweight children under the age of five is estimated to be over 42 million. The World Health Organization considers childhood obesity to be one of the most serious global public-health challenges for the 21st century.
- In the UK, one in every ten children aged between five and sixteen has been clinically diagnosed with a mental health disorder.
- In the United States, 6.8 per cent of children between the ages of three and 17 have been diagnosed with ADHD, 3 per cent with anxiety and 2.1 per cent with depression.
- According to the American Academy of Pediatrics, an hour of unstructured free play every day is essential to children's physical and mental health.
- The RSPB's Every Child Outdoors report found that 'there is very strong evidence that being outdoors is the most powerful correlate of physical activity, particularly in pre-school children'.
- The same report also noted that outdoor activities in nature 'appear to improve symptoms of ADHD in children by ... threefold compared with the indoor environment'.
- In 2015, the RSPB and 25 other leading wildlife groups called for 1 per cent of the NHS budget to be spent on using the preventative and restorative potential of nature to tackle problems like obesity and mental illness.
- 99.9999999 per cent of parents are nice people, just doing their best (according to wholly anecdotal, unscientific, but nonetheless probably spot-on research by your humble writer).

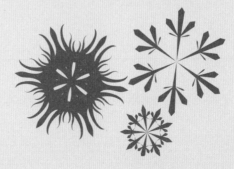

EVERGREENS

Sometimes, I feel there's a good case for taking winter to the Advertising Standards Authority for false marketing.

'Look!' I'd cry, jabbing my finger at the merchandising. 'In the pictures it's all crisp white snow, red-breasted Robins, icicles like perfect doilies and the warm glow of fires.' And then, to clinch the deal, my Judge Judy moment: an expansive gesture that takes in grey puddles on my grey street; the unremitting tedium of the unwaveringly grey sky; the grey slush – as if a manic depressive painter had mixed 'soft snow' with 'fetid fumes' on his palette; the grey pallor of vitamin B-starved faces, and the greying pulp of discarded litter that sits, soaking up a grey wetness that is so omnipresent it has stopped being a temporary state and become an existential statement: 'I appear wet and grey, therefore I am'.

'I ask you, ladies and gentlemen of the jury, does THIS look like THAT?' I would bellow, and they would give me my money back, plus a nice holiday in the Bahamas as compensation for emotional distress.

But it doesn't have to be this way. Over 10 per cent of the UK's land mass (11.6 per cent, to be exact) is made up of wonderful woodland. And within this enormous space the mighty conifer reigns supreme. An estimated 59 per cent of woodland is made up of this largely evergreen division of trees. And evergreen in winter means... green! Fresh, bright, crisp, optimistic, not-grey GREEN! All you have to do to banish the grey-blues is head to your nearest patch of woodland.

There is, of course, a downer. The green is shrinking. According to the UN Food and Agriculture Organization, deforestation was at its highest rate in the 1990s. Every year in the 1990s, the world lost on average 16 million hectares of forest. Even today, the UN estimates that 13 million hectares of forest are lost each year – roughly the size of England. At this rate, researchers predict that forests will decline from the 30 per cent of the world's land mass that they cover today, to 22 per cent within the next two centuries.

Building houses, factories, shops and motorways for us to use; intensive farming of food for us to eat; generating the energy needed to run our lovely lives and disposing of the whopping waste those lives generate... it all comes at the expense of trees.

And trees are useful, of course. They produce food. They give us medicine and warmth. They moderate the Earth's temperature and rainfall while producing oxygen and absorbing the dangerous levels of carbon dioxide that we humans have been pumping out since the Industrial Revolution. In the UK, where more than 440 ancient woodlands were under threat at the time of writing, they support a greater number of endangered species than any other habitat. Woods are vital to our wildlife and to our national identity but also, I would personally and passionately argue, in this small and subdued island perhaps above all others, to our winter colour palette and annual collective battle with the dangerous epidemic know as Seasonal Crossness Disorder.

FACTS TO FIRE THE IMAGINATION

- Holly has been used to decorate homes for thousands of years. It was traditionally thought to ward off evil spirits, particularly witches and goblins.
- Deciduous trees shed their leaves in order to adapt to cold or dry seasons.
- Evergreen trees loose leaves, too, but gradually instead of all at once.
- Most plants found in tropical rainforests are evergreens.
- Elsewhere, being evergreen is a response to low nutrient levels in the environment. Deciduous trees, you see, lose nutrients when they drop their leaves.
- Native Americans used the needles of evergreens for tea, chewed the pitch like gum, used the inner bark for food and medicine, and built homes and tools from the wood.

TOOLKIT TO TAKE

Scissors
Paper plate
Sellotape
Paper
Paints
Brushes
PVA glue
Jam jar
Needle and thread
Crayons
String

IDEAS TO START WITH

HUNT FOR COLOUR

Pull on your wellies and waterproofs, fill a Thermos and do battle with the grey: how many colours can you spot in nature? It might be a towering conifer in next door's garden, or a flash of red on a Robin's chest, a holly berry, a streak of blue sky between the clouds, a fern or an island of grass in a sea of mud. Make a note of each thing you find and its colour – the person who spots the most wins.

Note Try sketching your finds as you go.

MAKE AN EVERGREEN WREATH

1 Collect evergreens to decorate and brighten your wreath: holly with berries, pine needles...

2 Grab a paper plate and cut out the inside so that just the rim remains.

3 Arrange the evergreens around the rim.

4 When you're happy with their placement, tape them on.

5 Hang your wreath over a door knocker or on a wall.

MAKE PINE-NEEDLE TREE DECORATIONS

Stars

1 You'll need five long pine needles for each star, roughly of the same length.

2 Arrange your needles into a five-pointed star.

3 Use thread to tie your needles at every point where they cross (including the star's points, obviously). This is very fiddly, I'm afraid.

4 Tie a long piece of thread to one point of the star, then make a loop in it so you can hang your decoration on a Christmas tree.

Note If you can find red berries, skewer them onto the pine needles before tying them into the star shape, to add colour to your decorations.

Hearts

1 Find six long pine needles for each heart you want to make.

2 Bunch them together, then tie them tightly at the bottom (ideally, use a nice, brightly coloured thread.)

3 Halve the bunch.

4 There will be three needles in each half, so you can plait each one, tying them securely at their ends with more thread.

5 Roughly a third of the way up, tie the two plaits together with thread.

6 Now take the loose end of each plait and bend it back round to its base. When you're happy that you have a basic heart shape, tie them here with thread.

7 Hang your heart on a Christmas tree.

PRINT PINE-NEEDLE SNOWFLAKES

These make great Christmas cards. Or thank you letters, for that matter...

1   Go out looking for fallen branches bearing short pine needles (if this proves tricky, a snip from your Christmas tree will do if you have a real one).

2   Dip the end of the branch in white paint, then press its tip vertically down onto some coloured paper.

3   You might want to reapply the paint and press it against the paper several times to get a good impression of a snowflake.

4   For wrapping paper, continue until you've covered the paper. For cards, print the snowflake shapes at regular intervals so that you can cut it into rectangles and use them as cards.

MAKE HOLLY REINDEER ANTLERS

Another idea for Christmas cards...

1   Go out looking for holly leaves (be careful not to get spiked).

2   When you have a few, get out some colourful sheets of paper.

3   Draw a reindeer's face on the paper, remembering to leave enough room at the top to add antlers later, like below.

4   When you're finished, tape your holly leaves onto either side of Rudolph's head to make antlers and use a holly berry to make his nose.

BREW SOME PINE PERFUME

I'm going to level with you, we're not aiming for Chanel No 5 here. This is more for the kids who like mashing things into a pulp than for those with sophisticated olfactory systems.

1   Find as many pine needles as you can.

2   Stick the needles in a jam jar.

3   Add enough water to cover them.

4   Now find a good stick and mash, stir, shake and stab until you run out of energy.

5   Stick the lid on the jam jar and leave overnight.

6   Smell your delicious perfume.

Note Feel free to add other ingredients to the mix. We've even tried mud. It adds a certain depth to the fragrance, but I'm not certain it's one I'd recommend...

MAKE A CHRISTMAS-TREE COLLAGE

1   Go on a stick hunt. You need one long and thick stick, plus a selection of smaller, thinner twigs.

2   Use a brush to glue the big stick vertically up a piece of paper – this is the trunk of your Christmas tree.

3   Now for the twigs. These will be your branches of the tree, so you want to place them horizontally at regular intervals on either side of the trunk. Since you want the tree to get narrower further up, you need to snap the twigs into shorter and shorter lengths before gluing them on.

4   While they dry, gather up pine needles. You want short ones, ideally, since your tree is only little. You can snip long ones into pieces with your scissors.

5   Using the brush, paint a layer of glue on the paper between the branches in a pyramid shape (so that the tree ends in a point).

6   Sprinkle a thick layer of pine needles over the tree, then press down gently to make sure they touch the glue.

7   When dry, pick up the paper and shake off the excess pine needles.

MAKE PINE-NEEDLE BRACELETS

1   Take three long pine needles.

2   Knot them at the end if they're bendy, or tie them securely with thread if they are not.

3   Start plaiting the needles.

4   Knot them again at the end, or tie with thread.

5   Make a few more, then tie their ends together till you have a loop that will slide over your hand onto your wrist.

PRINT WITH FERNS

There's something about ferns that makes them incredibly satisfying to paint, then squelch against a piece of paper.

1   Go out hunting for ferns – woodland is the best place to look for them.
2   When you have a few, use a brush to paint them.
3   Lay the ferns flat against a sheet of paper and press down, gently, over the whole length.
4   Peel off the ferns carefully from the paper.
5   Now repeat, in different colours, to make wrapping paper.

Toddlers might find painting the ferns a little tricky. Instead, they can paint a thick layer of paint over one sheet of paper, press their fern into it while the paint is still wet, then press the fern onto a clean sheet of paper to leave its print.

MAKE A HEDGEHOG

There are two ways of doing this: the laborious but impressive way, and the easy and, erm, cheerful way.

Laborious but impressive Find an egg-shaped rock and a big handful of pine needles. Paint a little face on the narrower end of the rock. Behind it, slather on a thick layer of glue. Now layer on dry pine needles, starting at the back and overlapping them as you work towards the face. Remember that they need to be pointing towards the hedgehog's tail.

Easy and cheerful On a piece of paper paint the profile of a hedgehog, including a little face. Now cover the rest of its body in a thick layer of glue. Stick pine needles on top of this, remembering that they need to point towards the hedgehog's tail.

MAKE A PINE-NEEDLE PAINT BRUSH

1   Find a small bunch of pine needles and cut them to an equal length with scissors.
2   Gather the needles at one end, wind Sellotape around this end and voila! A paint brush.
3   Dip the loose end of the brush in paint and get to work.

Note You can try taping the gathered end to a stick if you want a longer handle for your brush.

BUILD A FERN DEN FOR A SPRITE

1   Gather five or six straightish sticks.
2   Using string, tie them together at one end.
3   Spread them, at the loose end, into a wigwam shape.
4   Push the sticks' ends into the ground so that the structure holds its shape.
5   Now cover it with ferns to make a shelter for a sprite.

NIGHT

It's 6 p.m. and the local park is pitch black except for the mini moons of the street lights that fringe its paths, the occasional shooting star of a cyclist's headlamp, and a galaxy of glimmering windows on the outer orbits of the surrounding streets. And, like a molten sun at the centre of this small solar system: a fire, burning in the grass, throws a yellow light up into the faces of a gaggle of young children – their eyes wide and fixated like those of little worshippers. Behind them the giant silhouetted arms of an electricity pylon tangle with the black, naked branches of winter trees.

When these children exhale, their breath crystalises in mushroom shapes in the cold air before their faces. But now they are holding their breath, listening. A storyteller spreads her arms wide, relating a tale that pre-dates the television shows that typically enthral them by about 2,500 years.

When we began our outdoor adventures, we explored on our own. Then, one afternoon, we saw a rain-smudged poster taped to a lamp-post advertising an informal, outdoor playgroup. Loosely organised by local parents, the group met regularly to do similar stuff to the things we'd been doing. In essence, nothing very ambitious, but outside, and in each other's company.

Most Tuesdays after school we took to walking down a scruffy canal path to a clearing where a straggle of local families would be running off some steam, having a makeshift supper and engaging (or not) in a relaxed activity. The adults drank tea while the kids – some crawling, some cantering – adventured in wide circles in a wild pack before everything and everyone was gathered up for bedtime.

The year worn on, the colours grew muted and the light shrank. The trees dropped their foliage and we put on layers; the grass grew damper and the kids a little taller. Otherwise, nothing changed. And now, here we all are, for the last session before Christmas.

The parents pass round a thermos of mulled wine and act as if the spell has only been cast over the children. But something about the wide open sky, the frost, the story and the sparks from the fire seems to transport us, if not to the past, then into some timeless zone. A place where – despite the occasional glow of a mobile phone, the passing cars and the cartoon characters emblazoned on backpacks – more binds us to all the previous generations who've sat on this scrap of grass than separates us.

We look at the kids, some still and intent, some wriggling, some poking the fire and some each other. We look up at the sky, dotted with stars and clouds, a smear of light pollution and aircraft. We look into the darkness and make out the shapes of swaying branches, old hedgerows, railings and high-rise buildings beyond. We listen to the story, our own breath, the honking of a horn and the wail of a child. And everything feels... okay. Balanced. As though it will, probably, be all right after all.

And then a child kicks off and the wind starts to bite, and we break away and head for our cars and our centrally heated, Wi-Fi-enabled, supermarket stocked lives. But the calm lingers in our minds for a while, like the ghost of the cold that stays on our cheeks well after we've gone indoors. It settles over the stress and the do-lists and the bills and the unfinished homework, like a wide-open sky putting the rest into perspective – until we feel the call of our next, snatched fix of the great outdoors.

FACTS TO FIRE THE IMAGINATION

- Most owls are nocturnal (only coming out at night), or crepuscular (active at dawn and dusk).
- Bats use a technique called echolocation to 'see' in the dark. After making a noise, they wait to see how long it takes for the sound waves to bounce back. That speed tells them the distance of all the objects around them (and stops them from bumping into things).
- Though hedgehogs' eyes are adapted for conditions at night, their eyesight is still weak. They mostly rely on hearing and smell.
- Only a very small number of birds sing in the night, including owls, Corncrakes, nightjars, Nightingales, and Reed and Sedge Warblers.
- Since light takes time to travel and stars are very far away from us, when you see the stars you are looking into the past.
- Only 12 people have ever set foot on the moon.
- We are made of star dust – every atom in your body was formed from the dust of an exploded star.

TOOLKIT TO TAKE

Paper
Pencils
Torch
Trowel
Card
Takeaway container
Magnifying glass
Scissors
Sellotape
Optional extra: hot chocolate

IDEAS TO START WITH

GO STARGAZING

Ideally, you need a clear, dark sky, somewhere far away from street lights, strip-lit shop fronts and office buildings that beam brutally into the nightscape. But for the small astronauts who dream of rocket trips from the fifteenth floor of a concrete jungle or the safety of their suburban semi, there is still plenty of hope. In the winter, when it gets dark earlier than in the summer, the possibilities to explore the night sky are endless. All you need is a clear night, this book, an outside space (a garden, park or even a balcony will do), warm clothes, hot drinks, imagination and sparkling eyes. Done? Okay, now can you spot any of the following?

■ the Plough (or Big Dipper) ■ Gemini ■ Orion ■ Cassiopeia ■ Pisces ■ the Pole Star ■ Venus

Note The night sky looks different depending on where you are in the world, but you can always find guides online. Wherever you stargaze, don't forget to look for shooting stars and other planets, too, and notice what phase the moon is in.

CREATE YOUR OWN CONSTELLATIONS

Sometimes finding the official constellations can be a bit of a struggle. Don't worry about it – try making your own instead. Does that group of stars over there look like a pirate ship, or maybe a Polar Bear? Can you see a train, or a Tiger? Is that a dragon, or maybe a dinosaur? Point them out to your friends.

LOOK FOR UFOs

At the time of writing, the website UFOEvidence.org (tag line: 'scientific study of the UFO phenomenon and the search for extraterrestrial life') claimed to have had over 7,500 sightings reported to it since its launch in October 2013. A survey in 2013 showed that 25 per cent of Americans believe that extraterrestrials have visited Earth. If you want to have a close encounter of the third kind, here's how to boost your chances.

1 Head to a hot spot. Stonehenge in the UK, Sochi in Russia, the Nullarbor Plain in Australia and Area 51 in Nevada, USA, are well documented for their alien visits. Otherwise, a garden or park will do nicely.

2 Have your close-encounter kit to hand: a piece of paper and pencils (for taking down notes and sketches of otherworldly phenomena), magnifying glass (to scour the area of signs of alien activity and prints), garden trowel (to dig up possible bits of space rock or UFO debris in the surrounding area), foil takeaway container to wear as a hat (it will protect against electromagnetic fields, mind control and mind reading).

3 Look for: strange lights in the sky, eerie noises, odd markings on the land and suspicious objects on the ground that could indicate previous alien landings.

4 Find a hiding place. Once you've done a reccie of the area, it's important to be shielded from sight so that any extraterrestrials aren't frightened off, and to avoid the risk of abduction or the theft of your hot chocolate by aliens.

LOOK FOR NOCTURNAL ANIMALS

There is a whole other world, right under our noses, whose inhabitants walk the same streets, sniff around the bins we use every day, and stretch out and play in the same gardens and parks in which we stretch and play ourselves. All you have to do to access this universe is come out after dark. Keep quiet, keep still and keep warm, and you'll see this other world come alive around you.

Don't use a torch or make lots of noise. You'll scare them off.

Do wrap up really warmly and listen carefully – you might well hear animals that you can't see.

Note You don't even, necessarily, need to go outside. If you turn off the lights in your sitting room and sit still you might get lucky.

What to look for

Badgers

Hedgehogs

Foxes

Mice

Voles

Bats

Moths

Owls

Deer (yep, even in some urban and suburban areas)

PLAY MOON-SHADOW TAG

On a really clear night, away from light pollution, you'll be able to see your own shadow cast on the ground by a full moon. Chase each other's shadows, leap on them, stomp on them, throw yourself down on them.

GO OUT IN THE GLOAMING

This time, when twilight starts to fall, creates all sorts of weird and wonderful shadows. Is that one a monster? Or a creepy, gnarled hand? Or just the neighbour's bike? It's like your own shadow-puppet theatre and you're in charge of the stories.

LOOK FOR MOON HALOS

'Ring around the moon means rain soon' – so the old saying went and, in fact, it's true. If you look up at the moon and see a halo of light around it, it's a sign that high, thin clouds are gathering up in the sky. Since the clouds contain millions of little ice crystals, the moonlight is refracted as it passes through them, making the halo.

PLAY TORCH TAG

You'll need at least four people for this game, and a bit of outdoor space with things to hide in or behind (trees, shrubs, lamp-posts and garden furniture are all good). Oh, and you'll need a torch, obviously.

1 Designate a target. It could be a pile of stones, someone's jumper, anything really. Place it on the ground in the middle of your space.

2 Nominate someone to be 'it'. They get the torch and the job of guarding the target.

3 The other players scatter and hide. Their aim is to creep silently towards the target, hiding behind trees and other objects on their way, and to be the first to touch it without being caught by the person who is 'it'.

4 Meanwhile, 'it' has the job of finding each player and 'tagging' them by shining the torch on them. When this happens, they are out.

5 If 'it' fails to tag someone in the first three minutes, they have lost the game, so it's a good idea to run around looking for people. On the other hand, if they leave the target unguarded for too long, a player might capture it!

6 The first person to reach the target (or the last to be tagged, if no one does), is the winner. They get to be 'it' next.

MAKE SHADOW PUPPETS

1 Draw the basic outlines of some nocturnal creatures onto a piece of card. Before it gets dark, or else by torchlight, cut them out.

2 Find some sticks and Sellotape them to the backs of the animals.

3 Hold them up against a tree trunk, wall, fence or the ground, and shine a torch on them to project shadows onto the surface. Make the the puppets hop around, play together, fight, adventure, nibble on leaves... whatever theatrics your imagination dictates.

SPOT 'THE WINTER CIRCLE'

Also sometimes called 'the winter hexagon', it's a big circle of eight bright stars, high up in the dome of the winter sky. It's not officially a constellation since only the International Astronomical Union can grant that illustrious title (and it has only, so far, deigned to recognise 88 constellations). Instead, it's an asterism – a recognisable star pattern – a rebel in the astrological world.

TRY THE 'YOGA' STAR POSE

1 Stand with your feet planted wide apart and facing forwards.

2 Breathe in slowly and deeply, then breathe out.

3 Stretch out your arms to either side, so they are level with your shoulders.

4 Breathe deeply.

TELL A STORY BY TORCHLIGHT

Clearly this is more authentically and cosily undertaken by firelight. You can't, after all, toast marshmallows on a battery-operated torch. If you are good at building fires and have, to hand, the space in which to do so and the materials with which to do so, I applaud you. If you're like me, use a torch and eat chocolate instead. Reading aloud in the outdoors is pretty magical whatever the light source.

1   Find a sheltered space in which to make yourself comfortable. This could be a bench, a fallen tree, a log, some garden chairs or a cushion on a balcony.

2   Sit down with friends or family, warm clothes, sustenance, a torch and either a book or a story in someone's head.

3   Nominate someone to tell the story. They get the torch, of course, with which to read and gesture.

Note You can also pass a book around the circle, so that everybody reads a page, or make up a story together, so that each person adds a sentence in turn.

TRY THE CRESCENT MOON 'YOGA' POSE

1 Stand up straight with your feet together and arms by your sides.

2 Breathe in and lift up your arms, straight above your head with the palms touching.

3 Breathe out and bend gently to the right from the waist, so that your arms point over your right shoulder. Don't push far – a slight bend is fine.

4 Breathe in, and bring your arms straight up over your head again.

5 Breathe out, and bend in the other direction.

WISH ON A STAR

1 Sit down somewhere very comfortable, where you have a good view of the sky.

2 Think hard about the things you want more than anything else. Go through your list carefully, examining your reasons for each, then pick your greatest wish.

3 Look up at the night sky and find the star that is shining brighter than all the others.

4 Focus intently on the star, so that everything else around it melts away.

5 Now make your wish.

PUDDLES AND RAIN

It was drizzling, a thin mist was hanging in the air, and I was running through dark, damp trees from the shadowy figure of a hooded teenager. I was tripping on branches and wet leaves, and splashing through puddles, the sound of my own ragged breath drowning out the cars on the main road just out of sight. My sleeve caught on a branch. My assailant screamed, 'I'm gonna get you!' and suddenly, there he was, his hand closing around my jacket and we both stumbled, laughing hysterically, into a wet tree trunk.

'You're my prisoner now, Miss! You've got to follow me back to base, yeah?'

I was in an area with one of the highest murder and weapons crime rates in the country. And this teenager was, officially, a troubled one. But this was a therapeutic session, run by Kids Company, an extraordinary charity that, before its closure in August 2015, provided practical, emotional and educational support to 36,000 vulnerable inner-city children across the UK, including the most deprived and at risk, whose parents were unable to care for them due to their own practical and emotional challenges.

The 15 teenagers who played a rudimentary game of 'capture the flag' in the woods on that wet afternoon had all been referred by their school. Once a week, for a total of 12 weeks, they spent a full school day in the woods.

'Nature is very important for children,' Camila Batmanghelidjh, CBE, the colourful founder of Kids Company, told me, 'because it gives them a visceral understanding of the ebbs and flows of life, growth, loss and regeneration, which concrete objects, like toys, won't give them. Children who've had time away in nature through our programmes have benefitted hugely. Some have given up substance abuse, others have gone on to follow careers in nature.'

'I love it,' agreed a small 13-year-old boy, drowning in the waterproof jacket he has borrowed from a Kids Company member of staff. 'I don't really have anywhere to go outdoors when I'm at home so I just like the feeling of space. He loves lighting the fire,' he said, gesturing with a stick to another boy, 'That one, over there, loves getting muddy, she loves finding things... Those two didn't even know each other when we started. Now they're, like, best friends.'

The group had stretched a piece of tarpaulin between two trees to keep the rain off the fire, on which bubbled some herbal tea that the boys eyed dubiously.

'Lots of them were very suspicious of the outdoors when we started a couple of weeks ago, and some had... teething problems at the start,' said Katharine Slater, who was Kids Company's Forest School practitioner, and you got the impression from her tone that she was making a very diplomatic understatement.

'Try this, Miss!' a trio of bright-eyed boys egged me on excitedly. 'It's a stinging nettle! But if you hold it by the leaf and squidge it up like this you can eat it! It's all right!' They balled up the leaves and chewed on them themselves. 'And this! Try this!' They thrust a sloe at me. 'It's a berry. If you eat it, it makes your mouth bare dry!' 'That's gross, man!' They dissolved into laughter.

Alongside the therapeutic benefits of the sessions, Katharine told me the children were working towards a John Muir Award, an environmental scheme that encourages awareness of and responsibility for the natural world. Anyone over the age of eight can enrol and take part, whether in their garden or on a wild mountaintop.

'Do you mind the rain and the cold?' Iasked some of the kids. They looked blank. 'What? Oh, no,' answered one, as if he hadn't been aware of it until now. 'It's fine.' And off they went, racing through the mud.

These were not 'problem' kids. Undoubtedly, something – no, *things* – had gone horribly wrong for them. There were problems here, lurking on the fringes of this forest like the evil stepmothers from old fairytales, waiting to collect the children as they stepped out of this haven and back into the world at the end of the day. But those problems are outside, in our wider society, not within the children themselves.

There in the trees that day they weren't difficult, dull or despondent. Not angsty, apathetic or aggressive. They were bright and brilliant, brimming with enthusiasm and infinite potential. Out there, with nature, each other and the staff, they were charming and chatty, enterprising and empathetic.

Given the space to express themselves, they were wonderful. Moreover (I'll hazard a cliché here because, in an increasingly urban world, it is poignant), they are our future. Not many kids in their situation get this respite. But this little

glimpse of the future, a one wet afternoon, was bright. Even when was is drizzling.

IDEAS TO START WITH

STAGE A PUDDLE SEA BATTLE

The best way of propelling a family off the sofa and into the cold.

1 Make your boats. I suggest a length of bark (body of boat), skewered in the middle by a small, straightish twig (mast) with a leaf pushed through it in two places (sail). But do customise yours in any way that you think will give it the edge in battle.

2 When your battle ships are ready, find a really good, big puddle on which to float them.

3 Set them down at opposite ends of the puddle, then, on the count of three, use all your puff to blow them towards each other.

4 Keep colliding them until one sinks or sustains such serious damage that it is deemed unseaworthy.

MAKE PUDDLE OR RAINWATER ART

I've included two methods here, one for the meticulous and one for the messy. Personally, we only ever use one of these. I'll leave you to guess which.

The meticulous

1 When you see the rain starting, rush out and put some pots or jam jars outside to collect the water.

2 When you've collected a decent amount of water in each, add different colours of food dye and swirl with a stick.

3 Now use a brush and paper to create a work of art.

The messy

1 Find a small, shallow puddle that's not too muddy (those on pavements, pathways or patios are best).

2 Add lots of food dye and swirl with a stick.

3 Now... SPLASH! With all your might.

4 See what abstract masterpiece you've created around your puddle.

Note Always use natural food dye so that it washes straight off.

Alternatively....

If you don't have food dye to hand, find a really muddy puddle, mix it up thoroughly with a good stick, then dip your brush into it and paint directly onto paper.

Or....

Put some thick paper outside on a flat surface while it's raining (hold it down with a few pebbles if there's a breeze). Dot drops of food colouring across its surface, then head for cover. Return after a few minutes to see what patterns the rain has made.

HOLD A SPLASHING COMPETITION

1 Find a number of really big, really muddy puddles.

2 Give them a good stir with a stick so that the mud mixes in.

3 Get each contender to stand on the edge of their puddle.

4 On the count of three, each contestant jumps as dramatically as possible into the middle of their puddle.

5 Whoever makes the biggest splash wins (you can test this more scientifically by measuring the distance between the edge of the puddle and the marks made by their muddy splashes.

Note The 'Hokey Cokey' is also a lot more dramatic when performed around puddles. 'You put you right leg in'... splash....

MAKE A PUDDLE WHIRLPOOL

1 Find a deep puddle.

2 Stir it as quickly as you can with a stick.

3 Hurl in a little leaf 'boat' and see what happens to it.

OBSERVE A PUDDLE'S MOVEMENTS

Okay, I know this sounds about as exciting as watching paint dry, but bear with me.

1 Find a puddle.

2 Drag a stick through the mud to mark its edges, or mark it with stones.

3 Go away and do something else.

4 Come back later and see what's happened: if its rained further, the puddle may have grown and swallowed up your earlier marks. If the weather's cleared up, it may have shrunk, so that your marks are now on dry land. You can re-mark the edges if you want, and keep the puddle under observation for longer.

Older children If they're feeling keen, there's an opportunity here to talk about the science of evaporation and absorption.

FIND THE END OF THE RAINBOW

1   Go outside on a day when it's bright but raining.

2   Look for a rainbow.

3   When you've spotted one, try to find its end. There's a pot of gold there, apparently, so it's really worth persevering. Oh, and did I mention that some of the gold coins within it are made of chocolate?

4   Since it might take you a while, sing the rainbow song as you go ('red and yellow and pink and green...'), and try to find objects in each colour of the rainbow as you go (a red front door, a yellow leaf, a pink raincoat on a passer by...).

Older children Rainbows are, of course, created by the reflection and refraction (or bending) of light as it passes through water droplets in the atmosphere. This results in a colour spectrum appearing in the sky, since sunlight is made up of many wavelengths – or colours – of light.

BUILD BRIDGES ACROSS PUDDLES

What can you use to help you traverse puddles without getting wet? Find sticks long enough to stretch right across them, rocks to turn into stepping stones, pebbles that can be piled up into bridges....

CATCH A RAINDROP ON YOUR NOSE

Turn your face to the grey, shifting sky and feel the rain on your face. Catch a drop on your nose, then your tongue, then your eyelashes, your little finger, the tip of your welly boot...

MEASURE THE RAINFALL

Or how to be a weatherman in training.

1   Cut a strip of paper as tall as your jam jar.

2   Line your measuring tape up alongside it, and mark the centimetres on the paper.

3   Sellotape the strip of paper up the length of the jam jar (covering it entirely as it's about to get wet).

4   Leave the jam jar outside for a predefined amount of time (exactly an hour, or a whole afternoon...).

5   Retrieve the jam jar and, using your paper measuring tape, check how much water has fallen in that length of time.

MAKE A RAIN MAZE

1 Collect rain in a jam jar.

2 Use a trowel to dig a maze of channels for the water to pass through, compacting the walls of your channels as you go. Damp soil works well, sandy and dry soil less so.

3 When you're ready, pour the water into a channel and watch it stream through the maze.

Note If your maze is big, you'll need lots of water, so collect it in other containers too, from puddles and streams.

WORK OUT HOW FAR AWAY A STORM IS

When it's stormy outside sometimes it's more of a 'sit on the sofa and watch the weather from the safe side of the double glazing' sort of day.

1 Watch for a flash of lightning.

2 As soon as you spot one, count the number of seconds that pass before you hear the sound of thunder (you don't need a stopwatch, just use the traditional, 'one Mississippi, two Mississippi' method).

3 Divide the number of seconds by five and you have the number of miles you are from the place where the lightning struck. If you keep counting after every flash, you might notice that the storm is moving, either away from you or towards you.

Older children Here's the science bit. When lightning strikes, the air around it can reach temperatures five times hotter than the surface of the Sun. When that happens, the air expands quickly. Thunder is the sound of that expansion or shock wave. Since what we see as one bolt of lightning is actually several strung together, there is a series of these shock waves. That's why thunder sounds like a rumble. So: if the light and the sound actually happen at the same time, which travels faster – sound or light?

GO ON A CREEPY-CRAWLY HUNT

Worms come up to the surface when it rains. Everyone knows that. But it turns out that the reason for them doing so is actually a bit of a mystery.

Scientists used to think worms were coming above ground to save themselves from drowning in their tunnels. Actually, worms breathe through their skins and need moisture to do so, so they can't drown like humans.

Today, some scientists hypothesise that worms surface to migrate: they can move faster and cover more ground above than they can below, but can only do so when there's enough moisture in the environment – after rain, in other words. Others think that the vibrations caused by rain sound similar to those made by predators like moles, and that the worms are therefore running away to escape imaginary foes.

Either way, head out in the rain and look for these mysterious little creatures on unfathomable missions. How many can you count? If you follow them, what does it look like they're doing to you?

SNOW AND ICE

It's snowing. Soft, white, blankety snow that belongs in a Disney cartoon or a winter wonderland.

'I moved here from Jamaica when I was six,' a young black man called Dwayne Fields is telling me. 'The first time I saw snow I was seven years old and it was my first winter in this country. I remember waking up in the middle of the night, which was pretty normal for me at the time because I often had trouble sleeping.'

'I looked out of my bedroom window and I saw the ground covered in white. At the time I had no idea about snow so I was terrified – watching this white stuff fall out of the sky literally had me in tears. I was certain this was the end of the world and that the sky was falling down. I remember feeling very much alone. I curled up in my bed, under my covers and cried myself quietly to sleep thinking this was my last day on Earth. Salvation came the next morning when I woke to hear my sister yelling, "It's snowing, it's snowing!". That was the moment I realised there was a lot I didn't know about the world I lived in.'

In Jamaica, he says, he'd run wild, outside, all day. In the UK he was met with a small concrete backyard. School wasn't much better. Fenced in, with his horizons literally shrunken, he made some bad choices – although, Dwayne says, he wasn't given many opportunities to discover that other, better choices were open to him. He was stabbed twice in fights, then nearly lost his life in another. The boy he was fighting pulled out a gun. Standing a few feet away from Dwayne, he pointed it straight at him, then pulled trigger. For a moment, Dwayne was sure he had been shot. But as his attacker was pulled away by friends, he realised that the gun had failed to go off.

When he'd cooled down, he realised he needed to make serious changes to his life. So, with no experience at all of outdoor pursuits, he applied to join the Polar Challenge, a 350 nautical mile team race to the North Pole. An intense ten-month training schedule followed, with sessions in a chamber cooled to -15 °C (5 °F), wearing just a T-shirt and shorts. Then, finally, the race: 32 km (20 miles) walking and skiing across the Arctic every day, crossing frozen seas where land and sky merged into one great expanse, sleep cut back to just four or five hours a day. Once, with temperatures dropping to -50 °C (-58 °F), he found himself in three pairs of mittens and two pairs of gloves, yet still unable to move his fingers. Another time he looked up to see a Polar Bear and her two cubs. Finally, he became the first black British man to reach the North Pole.

Now, back in a wintry UK, he's planning his next trip, to the South Pole this time, and trying to inspire kids like him. They don't necessarily have to go all the way to a Pole, he says, but they do need to discover the outdoors. He gives talks to inner-city schools and has lobbied the government to encourage more urban children to discover nature because, he says, while walking and training in the British countryside, he has never seen another young black face.

Inner-city people feel like the outdoors is not for them, he says, 'but that's just because they don't see it.' Merely getting out into green spaces can, he passionately believes, open you up to different conditions, different ways of life. You can relax, focus, think about the decisions you really want to make. Plus, he says, it keeps you out of trouble and promotes collaboration.

Dwayne thinks that the key to unlocking the potential of urban teenagers lies in the countryside. Even so, he says, shivering, 'I still hate the cold.'

- Every single snowflake is unique. Their intricate patterns depend on the height, temperature, humidity and dirt in the air they are formed in.
- The highest snowfall ever recorded in a single year was 31.1 m (102 ft) in Mount Rainier, USA, between 1971 and 1972 – a total more than ten storeys high.
- The tallest snowman on record was built by residents of Bethel, in Maine, USA, and it measured 37.21 m (122 ft) tall. It took them a month to make it in 2008.
- Ice covers a little over 10 per cent of the Earth's land mass.

TOOLKIT TO TAKE

Trowel
Birdseed
Bin liner or tray
Food dye
String
Scissors
Yoghurt pots/plastic cups/plastic bottles
Foil takeaway container
Brush
Jam jar
Candle
Optional extra: furniture polish or hairspray

IDEAS TO START WITH

MAKE A SNOW ANGEL OR BUTTERFLY

In 2007, a world-record breaking 8,900 people in Bismarck, North Dakota, USA, lay flat on their backs in the snow and made angels on the state capitol grounds. Among them was Pauline Jaeger, who was celebrating her 99th birthday by making her very first snow angel. 'It's fun,' she said. 'I feel just like a kid.' The moral: don't, whatever you do, leave it that long. It's much too fun to miss out on, and getting back up onto your feet is a much greater challenge at 99 than it is at 11.

1 Look for a patch of snow large enough to spread out on.

2 Lie down on your back with your arms and legs outstretched.

3 Sweep your arms and legs backwards and forwards across the snow, keeping them straight all the time. Don't pull your arms all the way up over your head though, and if you're making a butterfly, don't let your legs meet in the middle either (it's like you're doing star jumps, in essence, but lying down).

4 Peel yourself off the snow and stand up, taking care not to spoil the pattern you've made.

5 Admire your snow angel!

To make it into a butterfly Find a stick and use it to draw horizontal lines at regular intervals all the way down the body, then patterns on the wings. Add long twigs to the top of the body to make antennae.

GIVE A TREE A SNOWY FACE

While making a snowman is one of life's greatest pleasures, sometimes you don't want to venture away from the fire for too long. Here's a speedier alternative.

1 Find a nice, thick tree trunk near a pile of snow.

2 Pack together a snowball in your hands, then press it firmly into the tree trunk – this will be an eye.

3 Make another, and press it into the trunk beside the first, making a second eye.

4 Do the same to make a nose, add a sausage shape for a mouth and (if your fingers are still warmish) try making some hair, a bow tie, eyebrows…. Add pieces of foliage to brighten up the face and add convincing textures.

5 Run inside and warm your hands on a cup of hot chocolate.

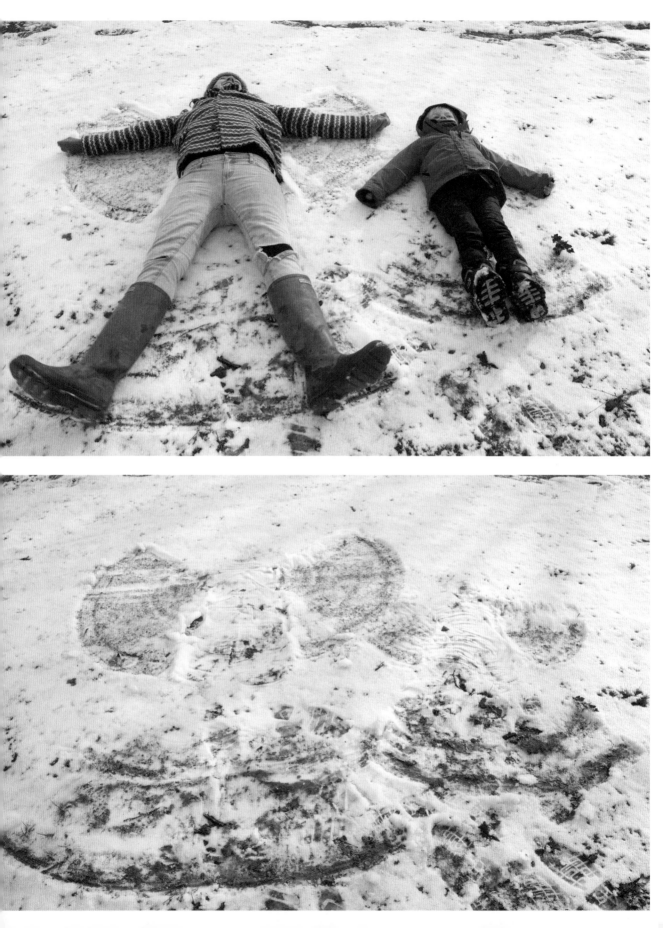

MAKE A SNOW ANIMAL

Because snowmen are *so* last season. Leatherback Turtles, on the other hand, are all the rage – and a Polar Bear pelt comes out lovely in snow.

1 Choose an animal to sculpt in snow.

2 Find a good spot – nice and flat, and near a good pile of snow.

3 Scoop up a few handfuls of snow and pat them together into a firm ball.

4 Roll the ball through the snow so that it gathers snow as it goes, getting bigger and bigger. Stop when it's the size you need for your creature's body.

5 Do the same for a head, paws, limbs... whatever you fancy, adding them to the body as you go.

6 Once you have the rough shape, use a trowel to dig, shape and draw more details.

7 Don't forget to make use of other materials – for example twigs for arms, horns or antennae, stones for eyes and noses.

Caterpillar Make six or more snowballs and line them up in a row, touching. Add stones for eyes and twigs for antennae.

Polar Bear Make three snowballs, one large, one medium sized and one small. The smallest will be your bear's head, so pile the balls on top of each other, with the largest at the bottom. Then pat two handfuls of snow into firm balls and place them on top of the heighest snowball, like bear's ears. Pack extra snow onto its front and shape it into a snout. Add two stones for eyes, and one large one for a nose. Use a stick to draw the bear's fur into the snow.

Turtle Make one large mound of snow for the turtle's shell and pat it down. Then make four small snowballs and arrange them around the outside of the shell, like little feet. Then make a longer, sausage-shaped snowball and add it to the front to make the turtle's neck and head. Add stones for eyes, then use the edge of a trowel (or stick) to draw the shell's hexagonal design.

PAINT THE SNOW

Because we love a bit of day glo. Because kids (mine at least) are not noted for their humility and so, for all snow's dazzling purity, we *can* improve on nature. It's just calling out for a bit of food dye and a manic artistic streak.

1   Take out some containers, be they yoghurt pots or takeaway trays. Pour a glug of water into each, then add different coloured food dyes.

2   Mix them up, then get to work on a smooth, snowy surface, dipping brushes in and painting onto the snow. If the colour is not strong enough, add more food dye.

3   You can draw, or write, whatever you like. The brasher the better.

WRITE IN THE FROST

1   Go outside early in the morning, when the frost is still on the ground.

2   Find a stick and use it to write a secret message in the frost.

3   See how long it takes for the frost to melt and your message to disappear.

OR... PLAY FROSTY HOPSCOTCH

Because a bit of hopping is just what's needed to keep you warm. That and a bucket-full of hot chocolate.

1   Use a stick to draw a hopscotch board into the frost,

2   Find a stone and try to throw it inside the first square. If it doesn't land within the lines, you loose a turn.

3   Hop through all the squares, leaping over the one your stone is sitting on. You are not allowed to have two feet on the ground at the same time, unless there are two squares next to each other. Then, you need to land both feet at the same time (one in each square).

4   If you step outside the lines, or on the wrong square, you miss a turn.

5   When you get to ten, turn around and hop back, picking up the stone as you pass it.

6   The next player takes their turn, exactly as above.

7   When everyone's had a turn, player one throws the marker onto the next square and the process starts again. The first person to complete the course wins.

Note Make sure to avoid playing the game on slippery ice.

MAKE A SNOW BIRDFEEDER

When temperatures drop below zero and gardens freeze over, birds are deprived of their usual diets of insects, berries and seeds. Here's one way of helping them out.

1 Your birdfeeder can be as little or large as you want, and whatever shape you fancy, as long as you can hollow out a 'bowl' at the top to hold birdseed, so...

2 Pack together big handfuls of snow, then roll the shape in the snow, accumulating more snow until you have a snowball that's the right size for your plans.

3 Add, sculpt and pack the snow until it's the right shape – whether that's a hollowed out snowman's head or an ornamental birdbath.

4 Packing your snow into a firm structure, use your hands or a trowel to dig out a bowl in the top.

5 Pour a generous helping of birdseed (or muesli) into the bowl and keep watch to see who comes to eat.

Note Your can also make an ice birdfeeder, like the one opposite, by following the instructions for making an ice lantern on page 231 and filling it with bird food instead of a candle.

BUILD A MINI IGLOO

1 Pack snow firmly in a takeaway container.

2 Level the top by running a stick horizontally across the rim of the container.

3 Carefully turn the container upside down and turn out your first brick.

4 Make more bricks, arranging them in a circle with a gap for an entrance.

5 Make a second layer, sitting more bricks on top of the first, but edged slightly further towards the centre of the circle.

6 Keep adding layers, slightly closer in each time, until they meet at the top.

7 Wait for a miniature Eskimo to arrive and make his home.

BUILD A SNOW FORT

Or: how to make the perfect shelter from which to launch snowballs.

1 Pack together several handfuls of snow, then roll them on the ground until you have a snowball that is at least as big as your head and compressed really firmly.

2 Repeat until you have six snowballs, all the same size.

3 Arrange the snowballs in an arc, then pack the spaces in between with snow to make a solid curved wall.

4 Now make eight smaller snowballs.

5 Place these firmly on top of your wall, patting and compacting them down, and add more snow between them to join them together and make another level of your wall.

6 Make ten even smaller snowballs, add these to the top and fill in the gaps between.

7 Finally (and this is optional) add a layer of even tinier snowballs, but don't pack snow between them. These are your ramparts – you can pop up between them and hurl snowballs through them.

HAVE A SNOWBALL FIGHT

You don't need me to tell you how to do this – unless, of course, you want to have the killer edge (I bet you're all reading on, now).

1 Find snow near the base of a tree or near houses or roads, since it's likely to be soft and wet – the best consistency for snowballs.

2 Use snow a few centimetres under the surface – it's prepacked by the layers on top of it.

3 Using your hands, pack snowballs to the optimum size – 7 cm (2¾ in), or slightly smaller than a tennis ball.

4 Make a big pile of snowballs.

5 Identify places to take cover – trees to duck behind, for instance – and leave an 'ammo pile' in these places (a pile of snow to pack into snowballs while you hide).

6 Remember to dodge, not duck when snowballs are thrown at you. Since snowballs don't weigh much, their trajectory falls faster than you might expect. Duck, and you might find your face splattered in snow.

7 Aim your first snowball slightly to the left of your target. Be ready with your next, aiming to their right, when your foe instinctively runs away from the first snowball towards the right.

Note Never aim for the head.

GO DIY SLEDGING

Because really, who needs a fancy sledge when a bin liner has a much racier, crazed-inventor-dicing-with-death feel about it?

1 Take a bin liner to the top of a slope. Make sure the slope has a decent covering of snow (otherwise underlying stones will bruise your bum) and that there are no obstacles at the bottom of the slope.

2 Climb inside the bin liner. Make sure it's pulled right up around your waist.

3 Shove off.

4 Use your hands to brake when you reach the bottom.

Note If you don't have a thick covering of snow, a tray will do a better job of protecting your backside from bruising. Always, of course, exercise caution.

MAKE A SNOW LABYRINTH

Flick ahead to page 244 in Sticks and Stones to refer to the instructions on how to build a labyrinth. To make a snow labyrinth, trace the shape into a clear patch of snow, instead of using rocks.

MAKE SNOW TRACKS

Find a pristine, untouched patch of snow. Hop, shuffle, skip, leap… What kinds of patterns can you make with your tracks?

MAKE ICE DECORATIONS

1 Go out foraging for small jewels: leaves, berries, nuts, whatever catches your eye.

2 Pour a shallow layer of water into a yoghurt pot.

3 Drop your finds into the water.

4 Cut a length of string and fold it in half in the middle.

5 Place the fold in the top of the water, so that it's stuck inside when the water freezes, and hang the ends over the lip of the pot.

6 Now leave everything outside overnight (or cheat and put it in the freezer).

7 Once frozen, use a tiny amount of hot water to loosen the ice decoration from the pot.

8 Tie together the two loose ends of string, and hang the decoration from a tree. When it starts to melt, birds can eat it.

MAKE ICE SCULPTURES

The north-eastern Chinese city of Harbin has been hosting the International Ice and Snow Sculpture since 1963. Undeterred by temperatures of -25 °C (-13 °F), ice artists come each January with their swing saws, chisels and ice picks, and work day and night to create intricate sculptures, some the size of houses. In fact, tthe only thing ever to have stopped them was the Cultural Revolution. A bit of perspective for when you're facing a 'fleck of snow inside a mitten' meltdown.

1 Take a variety of vessels out with you – yoghurt pots, takeaway containers, plastic cups and so on.

2 Pour water into each container, then decorate them all differently – some you might add food colouring to, others could have leaves, berries and nuts dropped into them.

3 Freeze them – either leave them outside overnight if it's cold enough out there, or stick them in the freezer.

4 When frozen, pour some hot water over them and loosen them from their pots.

5 Arrange them into a sculpture: balance small ones on top of big ones, make bridges and cityscapes, or a mini Stonehenge...

Older children can chisel shapes into sculptures with a trowel or a good stone with a sharp edge.

SMASHED ICE PUDDLES

While not an incredibly sophisticated activity, this is astonishingly cathartic for all ages.

Find an iced-over puddle, jump in it as forcefully as you can and experience the profound satisfaction of shattering the ice into a thousand little pieces.

MAKE AN ICE LANTERN

You need two containers: one large, and one smaller and able to fit inside the first.

1 Take the large container and pour water into it until it's half full.

2 Gather some pebbles.

3 Drop a couple of pebbles into the smaller container, then place it inside the large one. You want it to sink but not touch the bottom, so experiment by adding and removing pebbles until it's at the right level. Getting it correctly weighted can be fiddly.

4 Now freeze the container: outside overnight if it's cold enough, or in a freezer otherwise.

5 Remember to take the container from the freezer when it's dark outside (if you remove it in daylight, it's likely to melt before dusk which, clearly, is the time it will look best with a candle inside).

6 A grown-up should carefully pour some hot water over the container, then children can – *gently* – remove both pots and reveal the frozen shape that is between them.

7 You now have a lantern! All you need to do is put a tea light or the stub of a candle inside and watch it glow.

Note Jazz it up by adding food colouring or nuts, berries and leaves to the water before it freezes.

Alternatively you can fill this up with bird seed and use it as a feeder instead of a lantern.

MAKE YOUR OWN CLOUD

This is just magic. It's guaranteed to turn even the most reluctant scientist into a mini meteorologist. Just remember to take some warm water out with you.

1 Take some ice. Ice cubes are ideal, but have a go with sections of frozen puddles or ice you find hanging from branches and gutters.

2 Place the lumps of ice in a takeaway container and wait for it to get really cold.

3 Pour hot water into the jam jar until it is a third full, and swill it up the sides for a moment before putting it down.

4 Place the freezing cold takeaway container over the top of the jam jar.

5 Keep a close watch on the jar. You should see a mini cloud forming inside.

Note For far more dramatic effects, remove the container of ice for a second, add a quick spray of furniture polish or hair spray, then replace the container. Leave for 30 seconds, then remove and see your cloud rise out of the jar.

Older children Explain to them that the reason this happens is that clouds are formed when warm, wet air is cooled. The cooling causes it to condense into minute water droplets or clouds.

STICKS AND STONES

'Sticks and stones can break my bones, but words can never hurt me.' Well, fine. But you can't build a den with words, learn to tie a knot around a word, build your own labyrinth or tor with a word or play pick-up-sticks with a word.

Plas Madoc is a housing estate that regularly ranks on lists of the most deprived areas in Wales. It has, however, been made famous by a fenced-off former wasteland, bearing a sign that reads 'The Land. A Space Full of Possibilities.'

On first sight it's full of... junk. There are 55 m² (592 ft²) of old tyres, broken pallets, a shopping trolley, giant tyres, old tubes, barrels, some ladders, an old sofa and a scrappy rope swinging over a brook. It's also, though, full of activity.

Kids swarm over it, building dens, sawing and hammering wood, smashing up stuff and even lighting fires.

Three members of staff supervise at all times, but still, with up to 60 children turning up every evening it all looks a bit... risky. The kind of stuff that breaks bones.

Back in 2011, when Claire Griffiths, the Land's creator and manager, first got the funding to set up a permanent play space on the estate, she wanted to create something different from the typical 'fixed' playground. 'They're so static, the kids can't change them or make them their own', she explains. Everything here is scrounged, there's no monetary value attached to any of it. Local businesses donate things, like the old pallets... It's intentional. We found that once money has changed hands for play equipment, if the kids start to try and adapt it or work on it, the adults' instinctual response is to say, "No! Stop! That's wrong."'

Back then, there were territorial issues on the estate, 'If you were a kid from the top of the estate, you couldn't be seen visiting the bottom, and vice versa. We wanted a space where they could collaborate, where everything was created by them.'

So they fenced off the space, dumped the materials they had collected in their van and that was it. 'Day one was scary,' admits Claire. 'I thought, what if they don't get it? What if they come in and say, "Where's the zip wire?" But they got it. Straightaway.'

Nothing here is ever finished. As one swarm of kids builds a structure from pallets and plastic tubes, a huddle in another corner is smashing something to smithereens. Pretty much the only constant is the fire.

'They build one every night at the moment,' says Claire. 'But you know, we don't take it lightly – there's actually a 13-page "risk benefit assessment" attached to that. Everything here gets assessed for what benefits it will bring the kids versus what risks it exposes them to. The thing is, in society more generally, they are protected from every tiny risk, they're never allowed to try things. And there are much greater risks attached to that. They don't develop the skills, or they go off somewhere secret on their own to experiment. Here, we introduce them gradually till they can do it themselves easily. And yeah, the children do occasionally get little burns, but we've never had anything more serious that that. And they only get them once.'

'It builds their confidence,' she says, as she watches a little girl concentrating intently on a handsaw and a piece of scrap wood, 'to have trust placed in them. They're so proud when they've mastered a skill. It's so incredibly important to be given the space and opportunity to try, fail and try again. It's how we grow.'

FACTS TO FIRE THE IMAGINATION

- Stones (or rocks) have been used by humans for millions of years, from the earliest tools and weapons through to modern construction techniques.
- The Earth's crust is made up of rock.
- Meteoroids are small rocks that travel through space. Shooting stars are actually meteoroids that have been set alight as they pass through our atmosphere (these are also known as meteors).
- Birds use sticks and twigs as building materials, weaving them into their nests. Jackdaws love building their nests in chimneys, wedging the sticks inside.
- You can start a fire without a match by rubbing two sticks together.

TOOLKIT TO TAKE

Double-sided tape
Scissors
String
Paint
Crayons
Paper plate
Brushes
Magnifying glass
Takeaway container
Paper
PVA glue
Rubber band
Pen

IDEAS TO START WITH

MAKE A SUNDIAL

Sundials are as old as time. The Egyptians first used a pillar called a *gnomon* and measured time according to the length of its shadow. Zhou Dynasty China called theirs a *rigou*, while the Ancient Greeks had one called a *pelekinon*. Now you too can create your own, henceforth to be know as 'the paperplateclockinon'.

1 Start work at around 11.30 a.m. on a sunny winter's day. You want everything to be ready and in position by 12 noon.

2 Find a straight stick, about as tall as your paper plate.

3 Use the stick to poke a hole through the very centre of the plate.

4 Somewhere on the edge of the plate, write the number 12.

5 Find a spot outdoors. Put the plate on the ground and drive the stick through the hole in its centre and into the soil below. It should cast a shadow long enough to reach the edge of your plate. If not, pull up the stick a little.

6 At 12, turn the plate so that the shadow falls on the number 12 that you have drawn on the plate.

7 Go away and do something else. But remember to be back in time to...

8 Check the position of the shadow at 1 p.m. and draw the number 1 where it falls.

9. Keep returning every hour and marking numbers according to where the shadow falls.

Toddlers will need regular supervision and help to get involved with this.

MAKE A STAFF (OR A MAGIC WAND, OR A TOTEM POLE OR A MAYPOLE…)

Is there any other, single object that has been turned into so many different magical, mystical or unequivocally silly things as the humble stick? Not that I can think of.

1 Go hunting for the perfect stick. A wand will be shorter than a staff, which will itself be shorter than a totem pole or maypole. A wand should be good and straight, too, while a staff or a totem pole might benefit from some 'character'.

2 When you have the perfect stick, find the materials you want to decorate it with – evergreens, moss, bark, berries or whatever else you fancy.

3 Wind double-sided sticky tape around the parts of your stick that you want to decorate.

4 Peel off the backing, and stick your decorations onto the stick.

5 You're done! Now all you need to do is to stride around seriously while gripping the stick, cast a spell with it, or drive it into the ground, attach strings to its top and prance around it.

MAKE A BOW AND ARROW

Or... how to be a real Robin Hood.

1   Find a long, straight, bendy stick. It's important to find the right one, so pick up a few and compare them.

2   Get an adult to score a groove all the way around the stick at both ends (they can use the scissors but must be *really* careful of their fingers).*

3   Cut a length of string and tie one end around a groove, knotting the string tightly.

4   Bend the stick into a gentle curve.

5   Pull the string tight, and tie it around the other groove you've made, so that it holds the stick in its curved shape.

6   Voila! You have your bow.

7   Now you need another straight stick for your arrow.

8   Very carefully, make a very short, vertical cut through its end with scissors. Even a little groove will do (adults, this may be a time to step in).

9   Slip the string of the bow into the cut or groove at the end of the arrow.

10 Pull back the string and arrow until it's taut then... release!

11 Practise your technique by aiming at a rock, or log or anything else, as long as it's not an animal or another person.

Older children can try to make a point at the end of their arrow, too, by carefully shaving off the end of the arrow with the blade of some scissors until they have a point. Even better, use a potato peeler if you have one to hand.

* If your stick has knobbly ends, you might be able to wind and tie your string round these instead of cutting grooves.

MAKE A CATAPULT

1   Find a forked stick (in a Y shape).

2   If the top branches are a bit long, snap them down to make the catapult easier to handle.

3   Take a rubber band and twist it tightly, a few times, around one fork of the stick.

4   Pull the other end of the band over the other fork, and wrap it around until the band is stretched taut between the two.

5   Now find something to fire. A pebble will do.

6   Put the pebble in the centre of the rubber band, pull back, then... fire!

Note Never fire at people, animals or even living plants.

LEARN TO TIE KNOTS

If you want to make a convincing explorer, adventurer, pirate queen or ninja, some basic knotting skills are essential.

1 Find a good, thick, straight stick.

2 Cut a generous length of string.

3 Practise tying the string around your stick in the following ways:

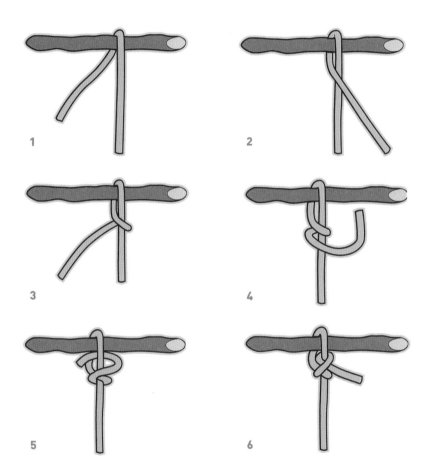

Buntline hitch Lay the stick horizontally on the ground and loop the string over it so that both ends are pointing downwards. Taking the lower end in your left hand, cross it over the other half, so that it points to 'four o'clock'. Now loop it back under the other half of the string, so that it points to eight o'clock, before bring it back over the top, pointing to four o'clock again. Now bring it up towards the stick and pass it through the uppermost loop (from right to left), underneath the stick. Finally, pass it underneath the bottom loop, pulling downwards to make a tight knot.

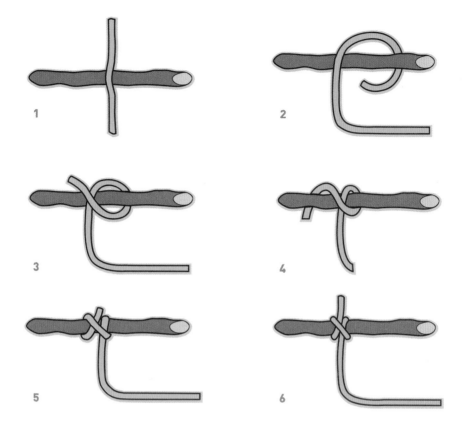

Clove hitch Lay the stick horizontally on the ground with the string lying vertically across it. Loop the string under the stick and bring it back up so that it crosses over the first loop (ending up pointing at 'ten o'clock' on an imaginary clock face). Now take the top of the string and loop it back under the stick. Both ends of your string should be pointing down. Pick up the end you were working with and bring it back up, looping it underneath itself as it crosses over the stick to secure it. Pull both ends of the string to secure it. It should look like a figure-of-eight.

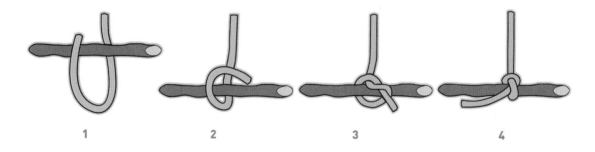

Overhand knot Lay the string on the floor with the stick crossing over it. Loop one end around the stick, then thread it through the loop and tighten it to form a knot.

BUILD A DEN

There are, probably, as many different designs for dens as there are humans on this Earth (but not as there are chickens – did you know that they outnumber us by three to one?). I don't intend to list them, or give you a definitive design. If you're looking for survivalist bushcraft, you've got the wrong book. No, what you've got here are some less onerous ideas for having fun in your back garden or somewhere else nearby, and getting home again in time for wine o'clock/children's tea.

- **Use a table** If you've got a table or bench nearby that's not being used, make it the basis for a den. Find long sticks and branches and prop them up at an angle all around the structure. Now climb inside, with the tabletop as your roof.

- **Use a fence or a wall** All you need are enough long branches to prop against it at an angle, and some rough foliage to weave between them to fill in the gaps and you have a kind of lopsided, ridge tent.

- **Use a tree** One with a fork in it, at around waist height. Find the longest fallen branch that you can, and prop it against the fork to make the den's frame. Lean other sticks and branches against this big branch, until you have two slanting den walls. Climb in.

- **Make it mini** Prop bark or twigs against a tree trunk to make a den for a sprite or small woodland creature.

- **Make it a tipi** Gather eight(ish) long sticks. Stand them up, then use your string to tie them together firmly near the top. Spread them out at the base so that they stand up without support. Push their ends into the ground to secure the structure. Now weave other branches through them to make walls (remembering to leave a gap as a door).

Note Do be careful while carting around large branches.

MAKE A GIANT STICK COLLAGE

1 Find as many sticks of different shapes and sizes as you can.

2 Clear a flat area of ground.

3 Now arrange your sticks into a picture – anything you fancy.

4 Accessorise your picture with stones, evergreens and anything else you uncover during your scavenging.

OR... MAKE A SMALL COLLAGE

As you collect twigs, look at the bare trees around you. Now use those twigs to make a winter tree of your own. Use one bigger stick as the trunk and arrange smaller ones above and around it as its bare branches. You can glue them to paper if you fancy.

PLAY PICK-UP STICKS

1. Go out and find twigs for your game. They should to be straightish and roughly the same length (so snap long ones).

2. Hold the twigs upright and in a bundle in your fist, then release your hand and let them fall to the ground in a mess.

3. The first player has to try to remove a stick from the pile, without moving any of the others.

4. As soon as they accidentally disturb a stick, the next player gets a turn.

5. Carry on like this until all the sticks are gone.

6. The winner is the person with the most sticks.

Older children can play a more complicated version where some sticks are worth more than others. To do so, they should paint their sticks in three different colours and decide which colour is worth 1 point, which is worth 3 points, and which 6. Now play the game and, when finished, count the points each player has collected in their pile. The winner is the one with the most points.

MAKE A STICK MOBILE

1 Find some sticks: one sturdy and long to form the frame from which others can hang, and at least four more. The more different they are from one another the better.

2 Paint the sticks. Stripes of bright, bold colours look cool. Or polka dots. Or animal prints...

3 Once dry, cut as many lengths of string as you have sticks.

4 Tie strings to the ends of each of the painted sticks and arrange them below the main frame, making sure their weight will be relatively evenly distributed along its length.

5 Now tie one last piece of string to the middle of the main stick, knot a loop at the other end and hang up your mobile.

MAKE CHISTMAS-TREE DECORATIONS

1 Find five straight sticks of roughly the same length and thickness.

2 Cut five short lengths of string and one longer one.

3 Arrange the sticks into a star shape.

4 Tie the points of the star with your string.

5 Tie one end of the longer string to a point of the star and make a loop at the other, ready to hang from a Christmas tree.

Note You can paint the star if you like.

LAY A TRAIL WITH STICKS

You can make this simple (a straight trail of arrows on open ground for the short of leg or attention span) or complicated (a twisting trail through tricky terrain for teens) depending on the company you find yourself in.

1   Find the sticks to make your arrows, pointing people in the right direction. You need lots: a bunch of sticks that are straight and long to form the bodies of your arrows, and twice as many shorter ones to make the arrows' arms.

2   Decide on your trail.

3   Lay your arrows at regular intervals along the trial. Make sure they're pointing in the right direction.

4   Find something to mark the finishing point with. Experience has taught me that a packet of biscuits is the ideal 'something', but any old 'something' will do.

5   Lead a friend to the starting point and challenge them to follow the trail. Time them if you want to add an extra frisson of excitement.

Older children can make it more challenging by getting their friends to jump logs, cross paths, weave between trees and cross shallow streams or puddles.

BUILD YOUR OWN LABYRINTH

1   You're going to need a *lot* of stones to mark out your labyrinth. So go looking for them. Large flat ones are best.

2   Think about the shape your finished labyrinth will be. It's a good idea to practise it on paper first (see step-by-step diagram opposite).

   •   Draw a cross and then draw dots in its corners, as if marking out an invisible square.

   •   Draw a curve from the top of the cross to the dot to its right.

   •   Draw a bigger curve connecting the right arm of the cross to the dot in the far left corner of your imaginary square.

   •   Draw an *even* bigger curve connecting the left arm of the cross all the way around to the dot at the bottom right of your imaginary square.

   •   Extend the bottom arm of your original cross shape till that arm is twice as long as the other three originally were. Then, starting from its lowest point, draw the biggest curve of all, all the way around to the dot at the lower left corner of your imaginary square.

3   Now try recreating the pattern in stones on the ground. It needs to be much larger, of course, so that people can walk through it.

Toddlers will need a lot of help from grown-ups to create a formal labyrinth. Marking out big shapes and patterns with stones is just as fun and needs much less supervision. They can start with squares, triangles and circles, then go wild.

MAKE PEBBLE ANIMALS

Can you find a pebble that's the shape of a ladybird? Or a fish? Or a toad? A giraffe? An octopus? All right, maybe not the last two…

1 Go hunting for interesting stones – what animals or objects do their shapes suggest to you?

2 Use paint and brushes to paint them as whatever creature or thing you think they should be – red body and black spots for a ladybird, scales for fish and so on.

BUILD A TOR

The processes resulting in the formation of the famous rocky outcrops on Dartmoor, the British national park, started about 280 million years ago. Fortunately, you can build your own in rather less time.

1 Go hunting for rocks you think will make good building materials for a tower. Wide, flat-topped rocks are best – knobbly and odd-shaped ones will be very hard to balance.

2 Arrange the rocks by size and start building.

3 You want the biggest, broadest rocks at the bottom for stability.

4 As you build upwards, experiment with different rocks to see which ones fit together best.

PLAY A TRACKING GAME

1 Learn the symbols on the opposite page and remember what they mean.

2 Split into two groups.

3 Allow the first group to set off ten minutes ahead of the first.

4 The first group needs to set the trail – finding the sticks, stones and grass and laying the marks for the second group to follow. Each symbol laid scores the group five points.

5 The second group needs to follow the symbols and try to catch the first group before it lays the final 'home' symbol to mark the end of the trail.

6 Round one of the game is over either when the first team lays the home symbol or when the second group catches it. Tot up the points team one have scored, then swap sides for round two, so that team two lays the symbols and team one chases it.

7 Whichever team has the most points when the second round is over has won.

Toddlers If you want to involve toddlers in this game it's best to wait until you have a decent group of different ages so that you can split the toddlers between groups.

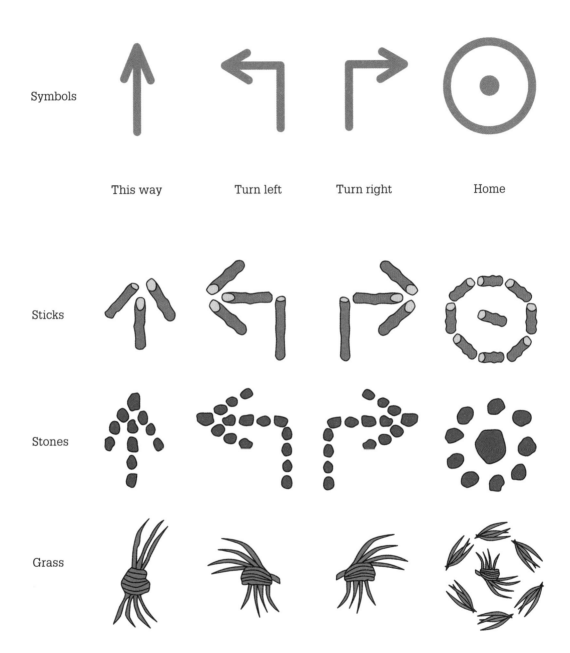

Symbols

This way   Turn left   Turn right   Home

Sticks

Stones

Grass

HAVE A STONE SCAVENGER HUNT

The challenge is to find as many of these as you can. Whoever finds the most is the winner:

- a flat stone
- a round stone
- a jagged stone
- a smooth stone
- a stone with a stripe
- a stone with a spot
- a stone with a hole in it
- a stone with a fossil in it

Note If you find a stone with a hole in it, thread it onto string or ribbon to make jewellery. You could paint patterns on it too.

MAKE A MOONSCAPE (OR JURASSIC PARK, OR A MINI ROCKERY…)

For all the astronauts in waiting. Or the time travellers. Or the more realistic trainee gardeners.

1 Find a collection of stones and rocks in different sizes and shapes.
2 Arrange them inside a takeaway container. If you're making a moonscape, remember to include craters on the surface. If you're catering for dinosaurs, they might want caves to hide in. If you're building a rockery, add layers of soil and look for little flowers or patches of moss to decorate it.

TOWER COMPETITION

Play against friends, seeing who can build the tallest tower from stones before it topples

GO FOSSIL HUNTING

Limestone, sandstone, mudstone, chalk, coal, claystone, flint – these rocks are all formed from sediments that settled at the bottom of a lake, sea or ocean, and have been compressed over millions of years, so the chances of an animal, plant or even a dinosaur footprint being captured in them, just waiting to be discovered by a mini Indiana Jones, are good(ish).

1 Look along the coast, in quarries, farmland, your garden – anywhere, really, where sedimentary rocks might lie exposed on the surface.

2 Pick up rocks that catch your eye and inspect them for fossils with a magnifying glass.

3 When you find a fossil, make a label for it, listing where and when you found it, what you think it is and what type of rock you think it is.

Toddlers With little ones it's okay to use a bit of imagination when identifying 'fossils' – rocks with swirls in them or with strange blobs on them could easily be dinosaur prints.

Older children If they want to be thorough, they can find fossil-identification guides online. The Natural History Museum's website's 'Earth Lab' page has pictures of more than 2,000 fossils and geological specimens, where they can compare their finds and figure out what their have.

MAKE A WISHING STONE

1 Find a stone that's full of character.

2 Write a wish on it.

3 Drop it into a river or bury it in the soil, and wait for it to come true.

RESOURCES

There's something a little ironic about creating a website with the aim of sparking children's interest in the outdoors – the better the site, the more time they'll spend indoors, glued to a screen. Still, there are a handful of websites that tread this tightrope with grace and skill, balancing fun and educational content with downloadable materials designed to propel kids away from the computer and into the countryside.

www.rspb.org.uk/families
The RSPB's family pages are an equal joy. There are dedicated sections for the under fives and over thirteens, as well as competitions, clubs, finger puppets, masks and word puzzles.

www.naturedetectives.org.uk
This fantastic website made for children by the Woodland Trust is completely indispensible. It is an online encyclopedia of outdoor activities, games and guides. You could explore it for weeks and never get to exhaust it.

www.50things.org.uk
Designed by the National Trust, this website allows you to tick off the '50 things to do before you're 11¾' (all outdoors) as you complete them, unlocking certificates, games and rewards as you go.

projectwildthing.com
This is more of a movement than a website. Still, the site is a good place to begin engaging with Project Wild Thing's plan to reconnect kids with nature. Watch the film, download the app, pledge to swap screen time for wild time and share outdoor ideas with other members.

www.naturerocks.org
Nature Rocks, from American charity The Nature Conservancy, lets you filter by time, location or weather to find the ideal activities to entertain the family outdoors. So there's no excuse.

Further reading

rethinkingchildhood.com
A blog by Tim Gill, one of the UK's leading thinkers on play and childhood.

richardlouv.com/blog
A blog by Richard Louv, author of *Last Child in The Woods* and all-round guru on the subject of kids and nature.

www.forestschoolassociation.org
For more information about Forest Schools.

www.tinkeringschool.com
For more information on Gever Tulley's Tinkering School (watch his TED talks online, too: www.ted.com/speakers/gever_tulley).

playingout.net
For more information on 'Playing Out' and how to organise street play in your neighbourhood.

www.playengland.org.uk
For all the latest research on kids' play and why it matters, as well as more creative ideas on how to get outdoors.

www.farmgarden.org.uk
Find a city farm or garden near you (if you're in the UK, that is).

woodcraft.org.uk/
The website of the Woodcraft Folk movement for children

www.childrenandnature.org
The Children and Nature Network, for American readers.

www.nwf.org/what-we-do/kids-and-nature.aspx
Another American resource, the National Wildlife Federation's pages for children and families.

web4.audubon.org/educate/kids
The Audubon Society's kids' pages are packed with games relevant to American birdlife.

AUTHOR ACKNOWLEDGEMENTS

I'm indebted to my fellow adventurers: Tom, Johnny and Frida (you make every experience an adventure I want to be part of) and, of course, to Barney, Ella, Jasmine, Morenike, Remi, Dylan, Indiana, Betty, Coco, Henry, Max and the confusingly named Monkey the dog, without whom this book wouldn't have happened. They say never work with children and animals. They are so right, but also so wrong.

I'm extremely grateful to all the people who allowed me to interview them for this book, and opened up their homes, communities, schools and workplaces to our anarchic family visits.

Thanks too to photographer (and wise friend) Nancy Honey for her genius in turning chaos into something beautiful and to Asimina Giagoudaki for trekking through bogs and over hills and creating perfect lighting conditions out of thin air while nine months' pregnant.

Julie Bailey and Katie Read at Bloomsbury deserve an award for their patience and skill. And, last but not least, to all the family, friends, bloggers, tweeters, Pinterest-board builders and second-cousins-twice-removed who contributed a sea of inspiration, wittingly or unwittingly... I'm sorry that you are too numerous to name, but thank you too.

PHOTOGRAPH CREDITS

Bloomsbury Publishing would like to thank the following for providing photographs and for permission to reproduce copyright material within this book. While every effort has been made to trace and acknowledge all copyright holders, we would like to apologise for any errors or omissions, and invite readers to inform us so that corrections can be made in any future editions.

Photographer **Nancy Honey** was commissioned to take all the activity photos for *Born to Be Wild*. With the exception of the photographs and images listed on the page numbers below, all photographs in this book remain © Nancy Honey.

11 © Hattie Garlick; 18 bottom right © Shutterstock.com; 27 top left © Hattie Garlick; 35 top right © Hattie Garlick; 41 © Shutterstock.com; 43 © Hattie Garlick; 61 top right © Shutterstock.com; 71 middle left © Shutterstock.com; 76–77 © Shutterstock.com; 88 bottom © Shutterstock.com; 93 all © Shutterstock.com; 100–101 © Shutterstock.com; 119 bottom right © Hattie Garlick; 132 bottom © Shutterstock.com; 135 © Hattie Garlick; 137 © Hattie Garlick; 142–143 © Shutterstock.com; 154 © Shutterstock.com; 157 bottom right © Shutterstock.com; 168–169 © Shutterstock.com; 170 © Shutterstock.com; 174 © Shutterstock.com; 181 top © Duncan Shaw/Gettyimages; 181 bottom left © Adam Burton/Gettyimages; 181 bottom right © Toru Karaki/EyeEm/Gettyimages; 186 inset © Hattie Garlick; 195 top right © Shutterstock.com; 211 © Shutterstock.com; 212–213 © Shutterstock.com; 242–243 © Shutterstock.com; 248–249 © Shutterstock.com.

The illustrations on pages 28, 39, 42, 55, 95, 136, 149, 158, 171, 175, 189, 238–239, 245 and 247 are by Dave Saunders and are © Bloomsbury Publishing. The swallow artwork on page 185 is © Ian Claxton and is reproduced with kind permission of the RSPB. All other graphics are © Shutterstock.com.

NANCY HONEY has been photographing for more than 35 years and has studied Fine Art, Graphic Design and Photography in both the US and the UK.

Her work has been widely published and exhibited internationally and she has received numerous awards. She is a Fellow of Photography at the National Museum of Photography, Film and Television. Her pictures are in many international public and private collections.

She has made many personal projects and her commercial work includes editorial, corporate, advertising and private commissions.

She has published 4 photographic monographs.

To find out more please visit http://www.nancyhoney.com

INDEX